EXPLORATION INTO EXPERIENCE

THE IMAGE OF LIFE

Brenda Lealman

and

Edward Robinson

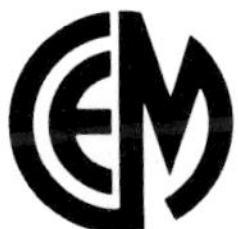

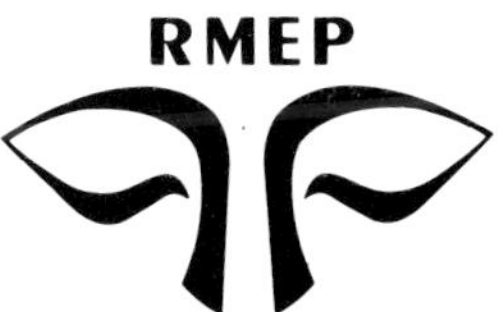

First published 1980 by Christian Education Movement.
Revised edition published by CEM/RMEP 1983.

We are grateful to the following for permission to quote from the works mentioned:

Messrs Faber & Faber, *Circle*, ed. Martin, Nicholson and Gabo; Messrs Harper & Row, *Beyond Belief*, Robert Bellah.

We are grateful to the following for permission to reproduce photographs:

Bureau Voorlichting en Publiciteit, Rotterdam; Courtauld Institute, London; Materials Research Laboratory, Pennsylvania State University; Staatliche Landesbildstellung, Hamburg; Tate Gallery, London; Whitworth Art Gallery, University of Manchester.

We are also grateful to the Hibbert Trust for a generous grant towards the cost of the original publication.

This series, *Exploration into Experience*, is being prepared by the Christian Education Movement in collaboration with the Religious Experience Research Unit, Manchester College, Oxford.

CHRISTIAN EDUCATION MOVEMENT
2 Chester House, Pages Lane, London N10 1PR
ISBN 0 905022-61-0

RELIGIOUS AND MORAL EDUCATION PRESS
Hennock Road, Exeter EX2 8RP
An Imprint of Arnold-Wheaton
ISBN 0 08 - 030630-6 net

INTRODUCTION

Art and Mystery

All living is exploration: exploration of experience.

The world we live in is full of problems. Most of these can, in the
end, be solved. Or at least we can imagine solutions, even if we
cannot ourselves achieve them.

But there are also mysteries: the everyday mysteries of birth and
death: the mysteries of the unpredictable energies within the atom
and of the endless expanse of space beyond us — that infinite space
whose eternal silence, Pascal said, struck him with terror; the
mysteries of human freedom, and of man's sense of good and evil in
an apparently random world.

Such mysteries as these cannot be solved — for what would count as
a solution? They can only be contemplated. And it is the
contemplation of these mysteries that has given rise to religion —
and to art.

To religion, because in a world that does not make sense man
searches for some meaning to his individual existence, and gives
expression to that search in religious belief and ritual; and to art,
because that expression cannot be articulated except through the
work of the imagination: through poetry, painting and sculpture,
music and drama.

The Work of Art

Imagination is more than mere fantasy, that 'pure imagination' which we sometimes contrast with objective fact. Imagination enables us to participate in the creative work of art.

The act of creation does not finish with the work of the original artist. "Two are needed for every art," wrote Ernst Barlach; "one who makes it and one who needs it." Naum Gabo, another of the sculptors represented here, says the same: "A work of art, restricted to what the artist has put into it, is only a part of itself. It only attains full stature with what people and time make of it."

So the artist (and with him the poet and the composer) invites us to participate creatively in what he has begun. We should therefore not hesitate to 'read into' his work ideas and feelings of our own. This is what art is for, to stimulate our own imagination, to set it free to explore our own experience. A true work of art throws us back to reflect on our own encounter with life. It challenges us into daring to explore the mystery which lies at the heart of all religions, a mystery to which they all, in their different ways, offer answers — answers, but no solutions.

Man expressed his sense of this mystery, his feeling for the numinous, through painting and poetry, sculpture and dance, music and myth, long before he came to formulate it in any creed or doctrinal statement.

Experience and Tradition

None of this means that we can do without the traditional forms of religion, or that the old symbols of the church are to be replaced. But all religious forms and symbols need to be reinterpreted in the light of each new generation's experience; only so can the truth they point to be rediscovered and so once more communicated.

We live in a so-called secular age. This does not mean, despite the prevalent materialism of our culture, that man's inborn spiritual hunger is now dead. What it does mean is that the forms in which that search is expressed are more likely to be secular than outwardly religious. So we believe that the work of the four artists represented here is an authentic expression of the religious spirit of this century, despite the fact that they do not for the most part use a visual language that is recognizably religious.

Exploration into Experience

Here then are four avenues of exploration: exploration into experience. But that experience will not only be that of the artists themselves. Each of these we have briefly introduced, and then allowed as far as possible to speak for him or herself. But it is not their experience that matters most now. They have done their work; now it is up to us, if that work is to attain full stature. "Two are needed for every art ..."

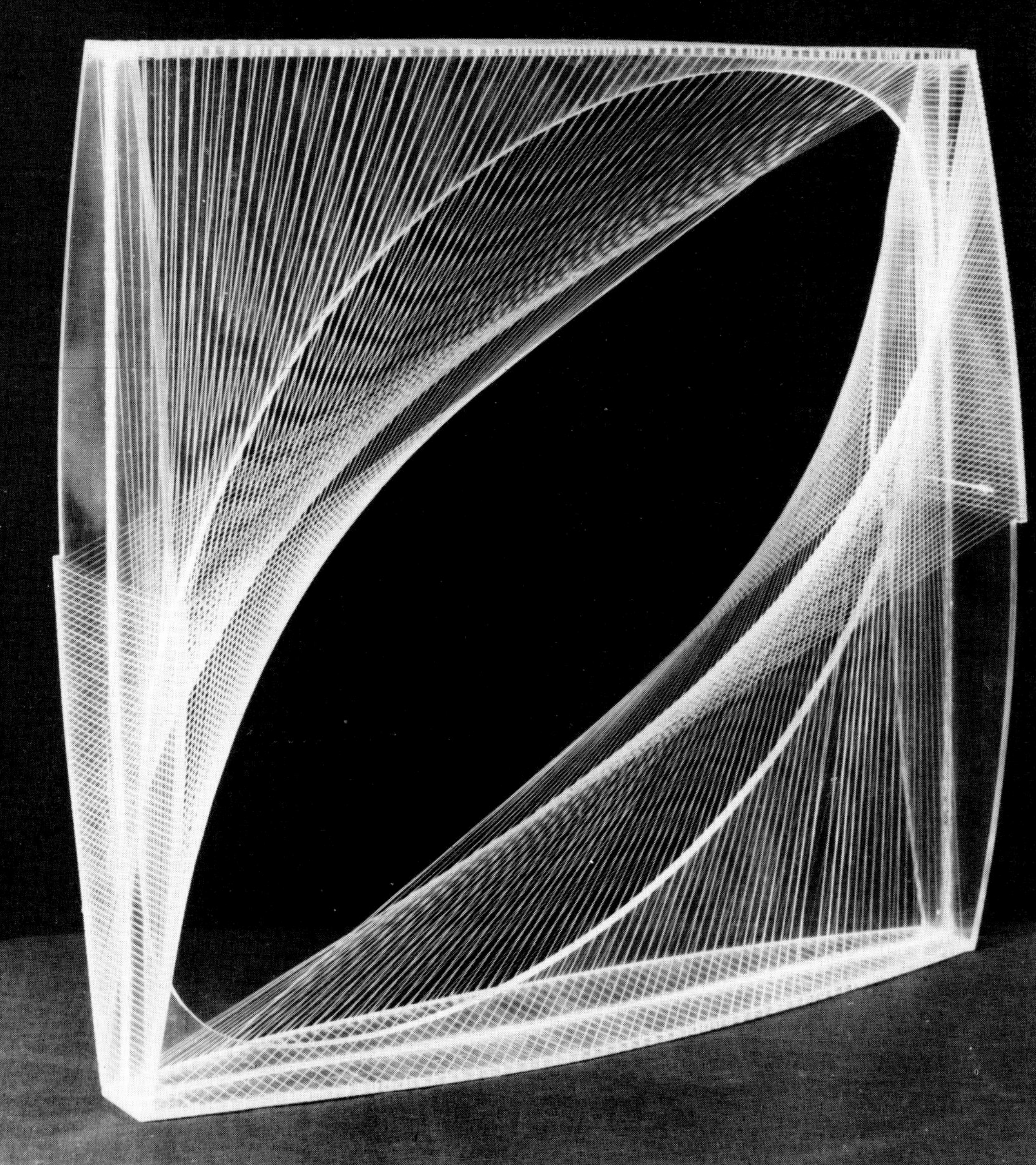

NAUM GABO

Art is an attempt to
transport into a limited
quantity of matter an
image of the infinite
beauty of the entire
universe.

Before we can prove anything to be true we must first imagine it to be possible.

Einstein once said that if it had not been for his feeling for the harmony of the universe he would never have conceived the theory of relativity. God, he said, does not play dice: the world, that is, is not a random mass of atoms; it is ordered, it has a structure.

Structure is what Naum Gabo's art is about. All his life he was fascinated with space. He saw the universe as an infinite field of inter-related energies, a dynamic whole which was still in process of creation. His early training had been in the sciences, and as an artist he devoted his life to the construction of models which would explore the mystery of space, and of man's relation to it.

But not least of these mysteries for him was the human mind itself that could conceive of these infinities. As he wrote, "We shall never have to undertake a voyage in inter-stellar space in order to feel the breath of the galactic orbits. This breath is fanning our heads within the four walls of our rooms."

To express this vision of the infinite complexity of the universe Gabo rejected the traditional materials of the sculptor — wood, stone and bronze — preferring to explore the new possibilities of plastic and other man-made materials.

It is a vision that is poetic and prophetic. His work affirms order, meaning and purpose. It also celebrates the infinite creative possibilities of man himself.

But these possibilities, as Gabo well knew from his own experience, could also in man be turned to destructive ends. He was born in Russia in 1890 and died in California in 1977. (He lived in England from 1932 to 1946.) He thus lived and worked through two world wars, each of which was for him a period of great spiritual crisis. The first for him was ended with the revolution of 1917—a moment of great hope for the liberation of the human spirit. In 1920, with his

brother Antoine Pevsner, also an artist, he published in Moscow the
Realistic Manifesto:

> Across the ashes and cindered homes of the past,
> Before the gates of the vacant future,
> Today we proclaim our words to you people,
>
> convinced that art must not remain a sanctuary
> for the idle, a consolation for the weary, and
> a justification for the lazy.
>
> Art should attend us everywhere that life flows
> and acts, at the bench, at the table, at work,
> at rest, at home and on the road, in order that
> the flame to live should not extinguish in
> mankind.

But he was soon to be disillusioned with the new Communist state.
Two years later he left Russia never to return.

The second world war was no less critical for him. How could the
artist justify the time spent on these visionary constructions,
seemingly so remote from the agonies of war?

> A world at war, it seems to me, may have the right
> to reject my work as irrelevant to its immediate
> needs. I can say but little in my defence.
>
> I can only beg to be believed that I suffer with all
> the world in all the misfortunes which are now fallen
> upon us.
>
> I try to guard in my work the image of the morrow
> we left behind us in our memories and foregone
> aspirations, and to remind us that the image of the
> world can be different.

I have chosen the absoluteness and
exactitude of my lines, shapes and
forms in the conviction that they are
the most immediate medium for my
communication to others of the rhythms
and the state of mind I would wish the
world to be in. This is not only in the
material world surrounding us but also in
the mental and spiritual world we carry
within us.

I think that the image they invoke is
the image of good, not of evil;
the image of order, not of chaos;
the image of life, not of death.

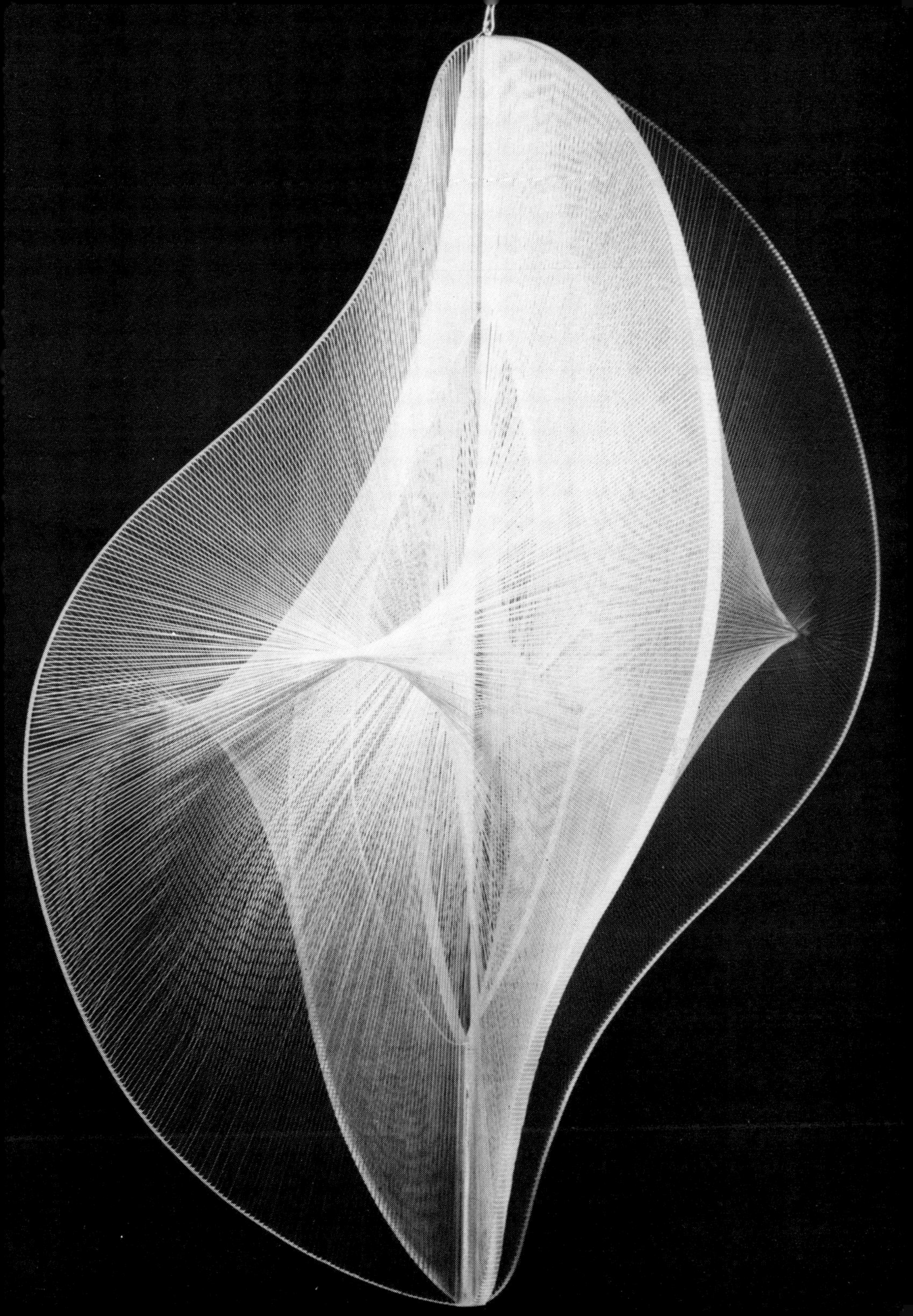

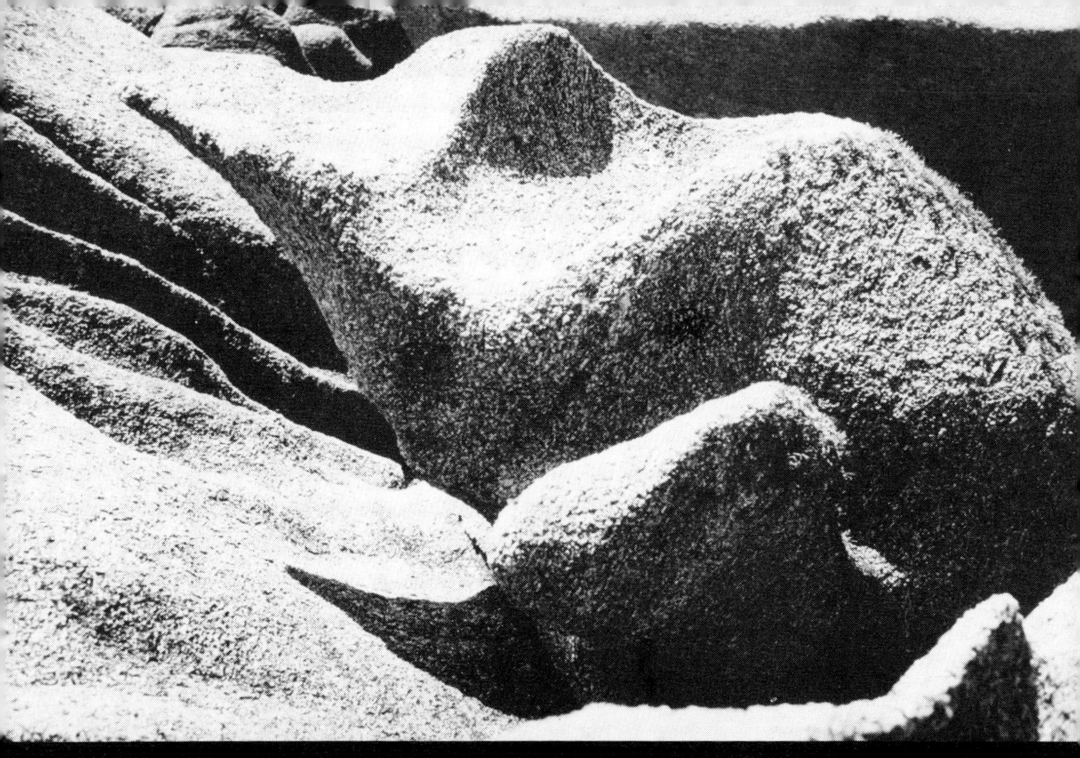

Where do I get my forms from ?

I find them everywhere around me, where and
when I want to see them.

I find them, if I put my mind to it, in a
torn piece of cloud carried away by the wind.

I can find them in the naked stones on hills and roads.

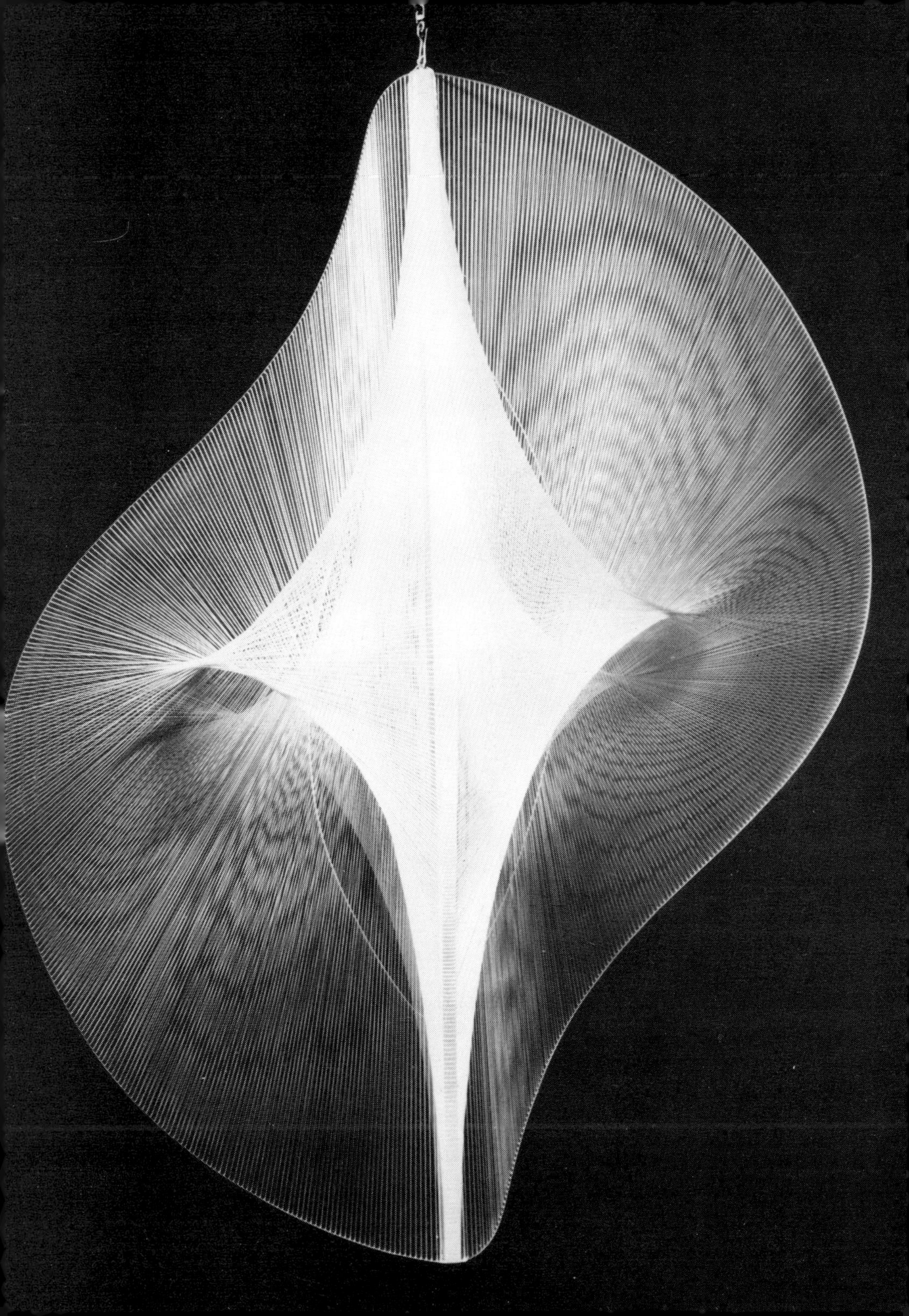

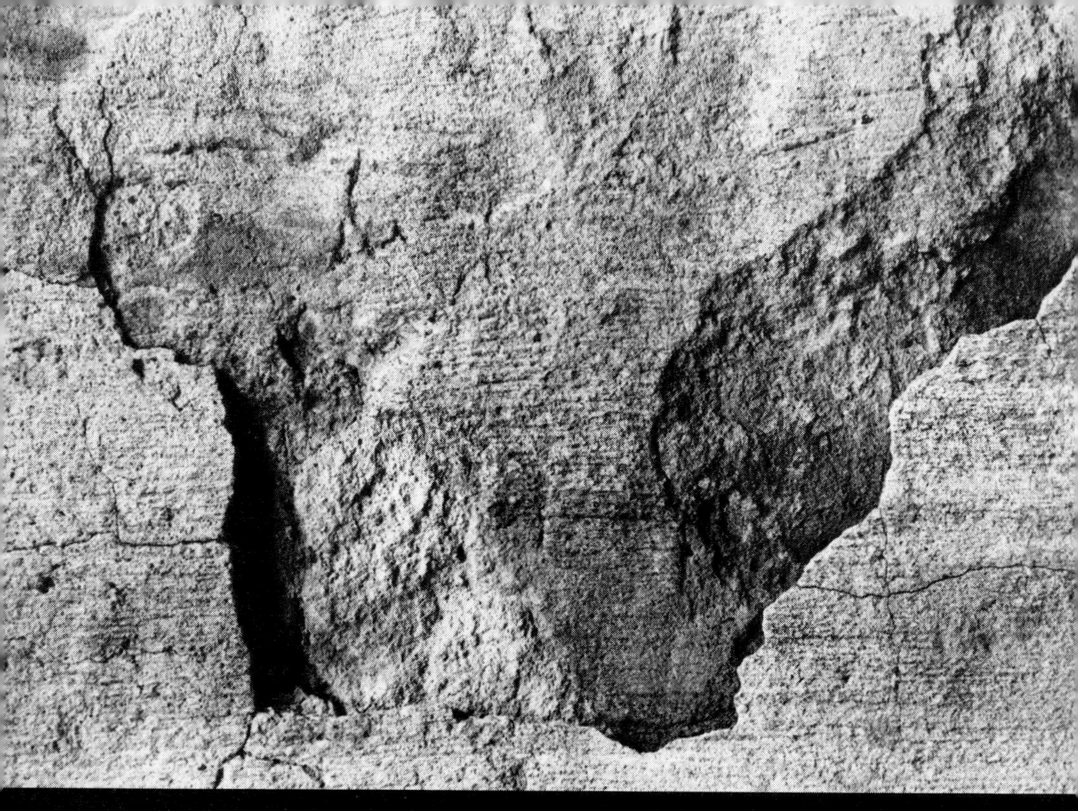

I see them in the green thicket of leaves
and trees.

I may discern them in a steamy trail of smoke from a
passing train or on the surface of a shabby wall.

Their apparition may be sudden, it may come and
vanish in a second, but when they are over they
leave me with the image of eternity's duration.

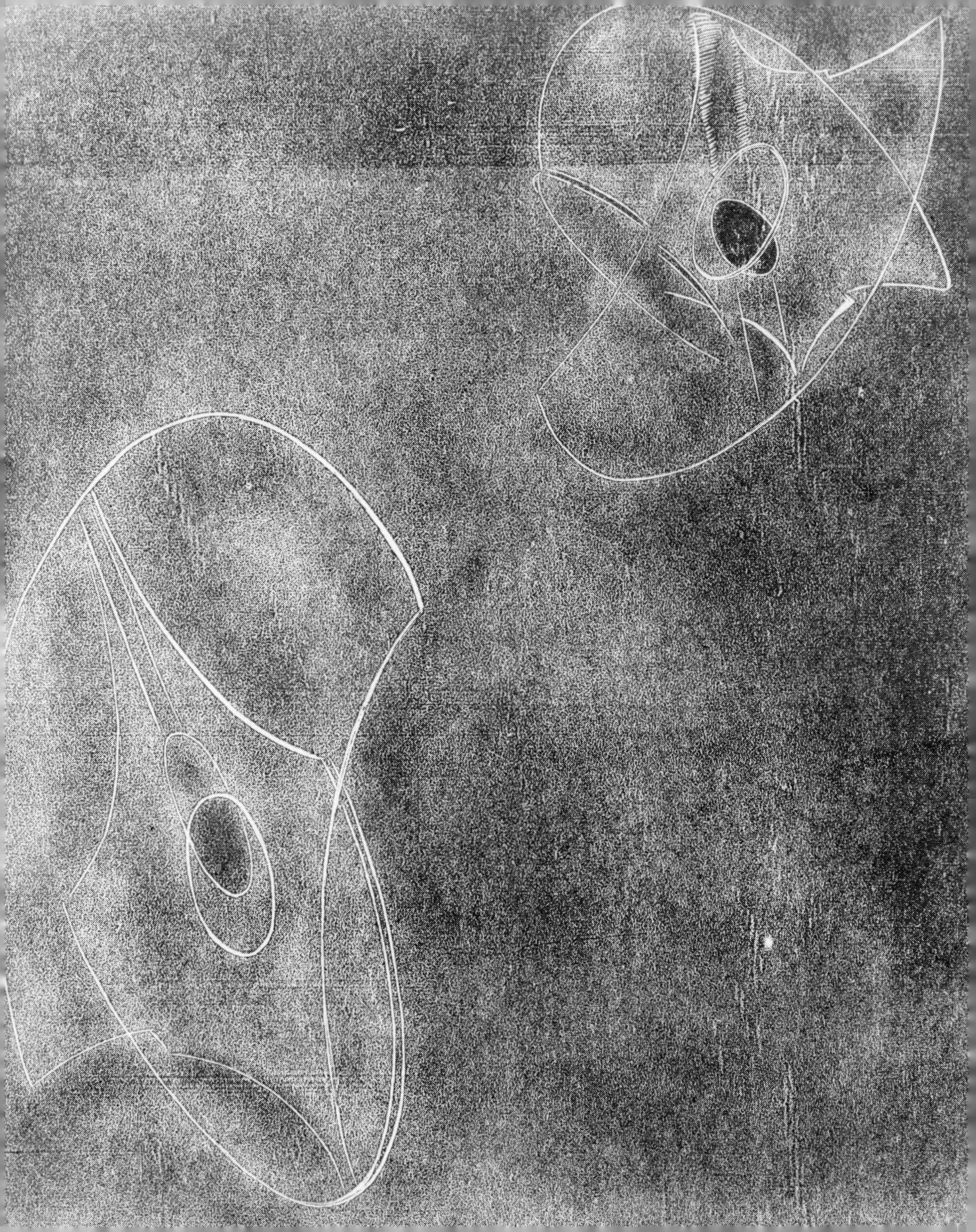

Sometimes a falling star,
cleaving the dark, traces
the breath of night on my
window glass, and in that
instantaneous flash I
might see the very line
for which I searched in
vain for months and months.

We all construct the
image of the world as we
wish it to be, and this
spiritual world of ours
will always be what and
how we make it.

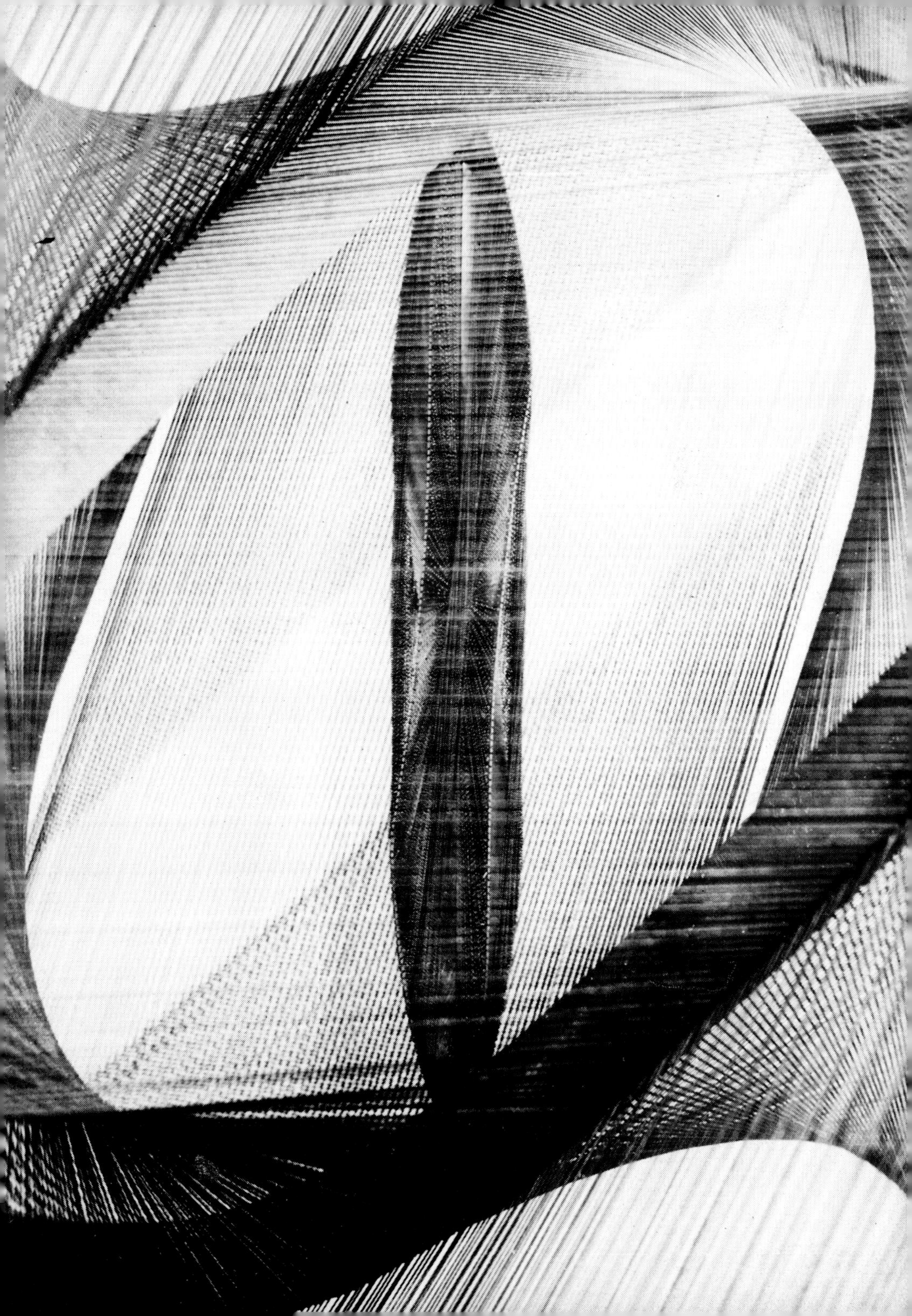

Day and night I carry the horror and pain of the human race with me.

Will I be allowed to ask the leaders of the masses engaged in a mortal struggle of sheer survival: " ... Must I, ought I, to keep and carry this horror through my art to the people?" — the people in the burned cities and scorched villages, the people in trenches, people in the ashes of their homes, the blinded shadows of human beings from the ruins and gibbets of devastated continents ... "What can I tell *them* about pain and horror that they do not know?"

The human race is ill; dangerously, mortally ill — I offer my blood and flesh, for what it is worth, to help them; my life, if it is needed.

But what is the worth of a single life? We all have learned to kill with ease and the road of death is made smooth and facile. Am I to be blamed when I confess that I cannot find inspiration for my art in that stage of death and desolation?

I am offering in my art what comfort I can to alleviate the pains and convulsions of our time. I try to keep our despair from assuming such proportions that nothing will remain in our devastated life to prompt us to live.

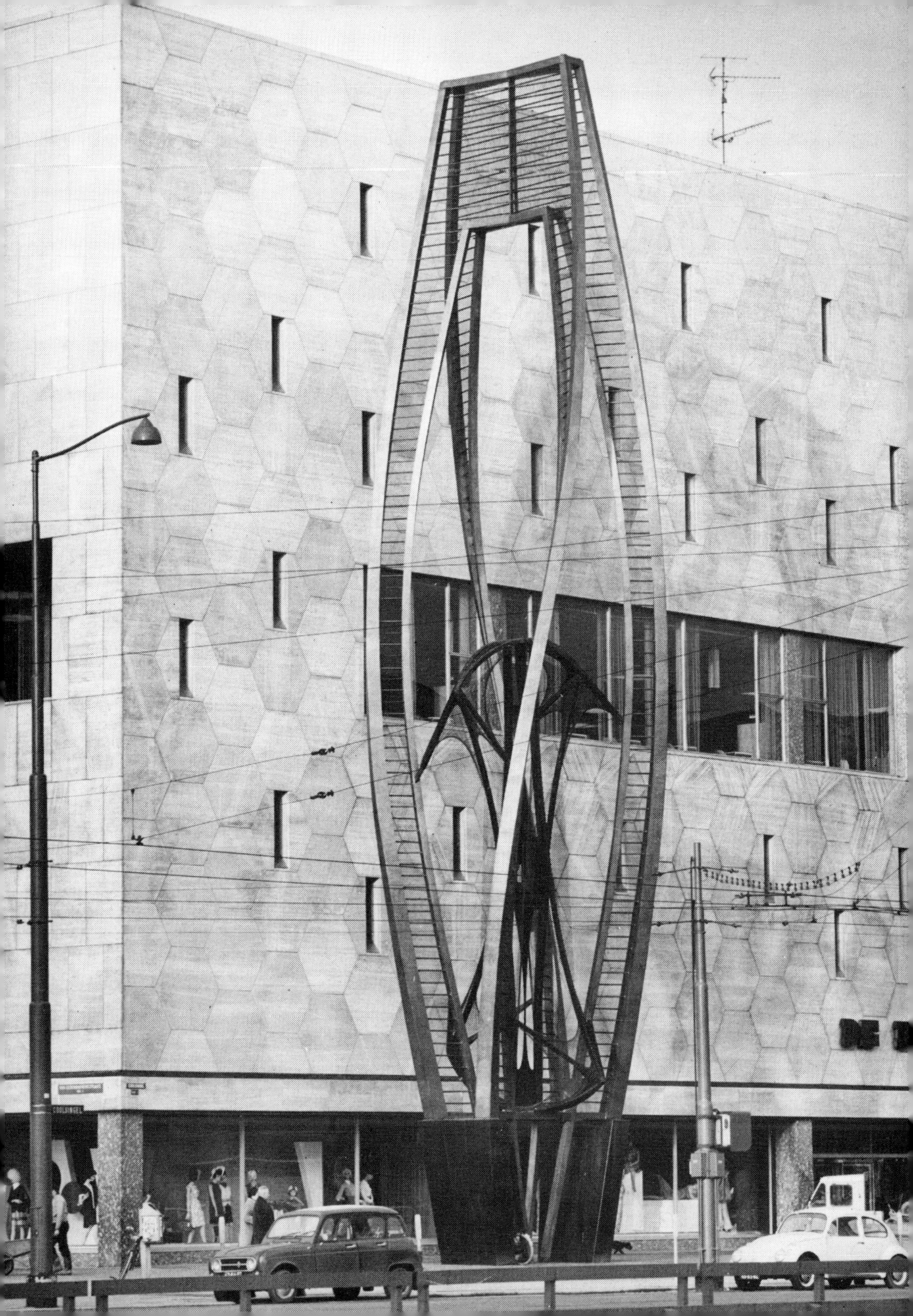

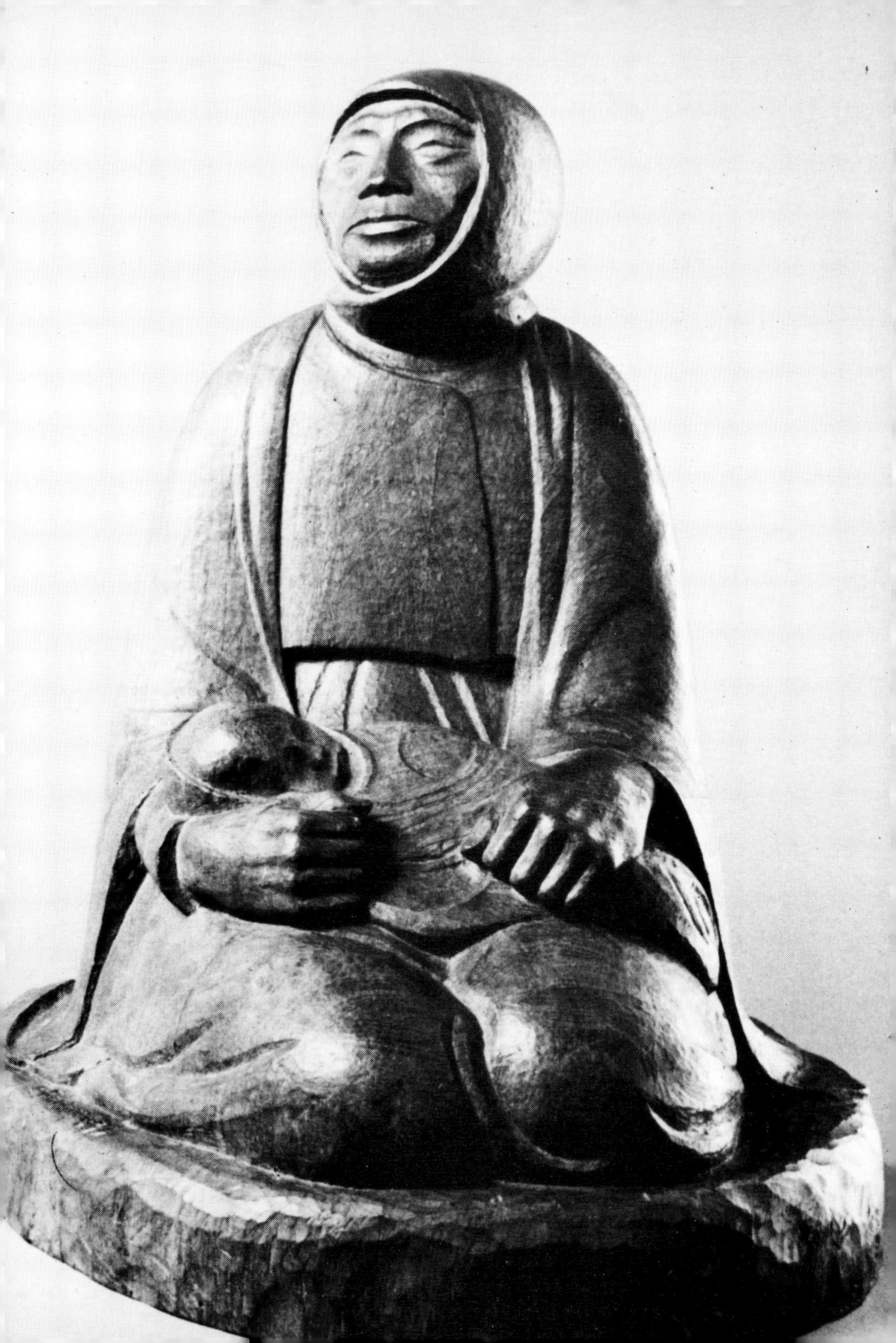

ERNST BARLACH

I can trust my senses not to betray me. Through them there comes a transformation of the spirit.

It is by a light that is spiritual and creative that I see shapes and colours.

Ernst Barlach was born in 1870 in the north German province of Holstein. He is thus the earliest of these four sculptors. His work is also, at first sight, the most approachable. Deceptively so, in fact.

Barlach stands firmly in the old tradition of German woodcarving that goes far back into mediaeval times and is still represented in countless tourist shops to-day. But it is a great mistake to think that because an art makes an immediate appeal it is therefore not profound or original. This tradition, he found, provided him with a language which enabled him to communicate most simply and clearly his vision of the world.

"My mother tongue", Barlach wrote, "is the human body, the milieu, the object through which, or in which, man lives, suffers, enjoys himself, feels, thinks. I can't get away from that."

It did, however, take him some time to discover that language. It was not until on a visit to Poland in 1906 he saw and began to make studies of the desperately poor beggar women in the streets of Warsaw that he discovered what he knew to be his true vocation. "I can bid goodbye", he wrote in a letter to a friend, "to everything I did before the age of thirty-six with a light heart." The human condition in all its joys and sorrows, its dignity and wretchedness, was to be his theme from then on. "I saw simultaneously the vile, the comic and — let me say it unabashedly — the divine."

Religion, however, he always found difficult. "I have for a long time now shied away from talking about God", he wrote in another letter, "though the word often comes naturally to me. But to talk about something which cannot be expressed in words, whether of literature or logic, in stone-carving or painting or drawing — this to me is intolerable." Yet in the wordless language of sculpture, that "mother-tongue" of the human form, he did find expression for a profoundly spiritual insight into the joys and sorrows of humanity, a deep tenderness and compassion.

Nonetheless, his sculpture was not generally appreciated in his lifetime. It was not considered suitable to be put in churches. It was condemned by the Nazis, who forbade him to show it in public exhibitions. In 1937, the year of his death, examples of his work were included in the notorious exhibition of "Degenerate Art", along with that of most other original artists then working in Germany. Why should this have been so?

To-day, compared with much other modern art, Barlach's sculpture looks almost conventional. Why should it ever have been regarded as politically dangerous or subversive? The answer perhaps lies in its extreme simplicity. All inessential detail has been stripped away from these figures, until nothing is left but their humanity. They appeal to us at a very deep level. To a totalitarian regime demanding absolute loyalty from the individual this was intolerable, because the kind of appeal made by this art transcends all political loyalties. It affirms an essentially spiritual view of man.

Joy as content, purpose,
meaning of the world ...
This idea has occupied
my thoughts beyond
time and space.

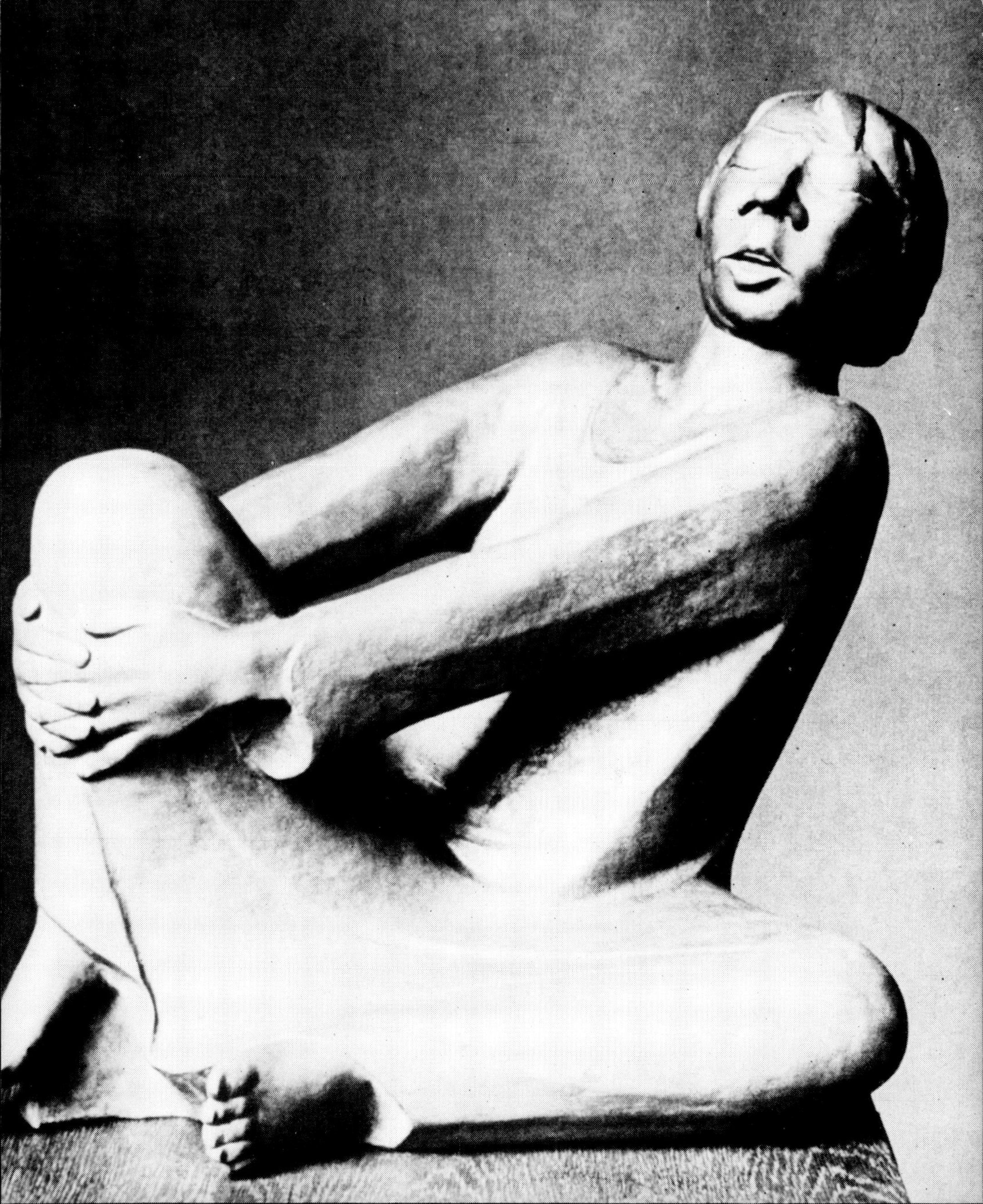

... It was as though my spirit was translated completely out of my body into a world of entirely new dimensions, a world in which time as we know it had no significance and in which for the first time in my life I felt completely and vitally conscious of everything which was going on about me. I seemed to be pulsing with a new and hitherto unexperienced vitality, and to feel master not only of my own destiny but of the entire destiny of the universe. Yet I as an individual ego no longer had any substance; I was part of the process of creation which was a combination of love and strength and humility, something infinitely gentle, infinitely wise and eternally at peace with itself. I felt a sense of complete fulfilment and yet of complete security, and the only way I can describe it is to say that I felt that I was part of God, part of His purpose and His eternal creative activity. There was no longer any light or darkness; I was one with eternally pulsing light, not a dazzling but a peaceful light, a light which was also love and safety. Yet I was not conscious of being safe so much as of there being no longer anything to fear.

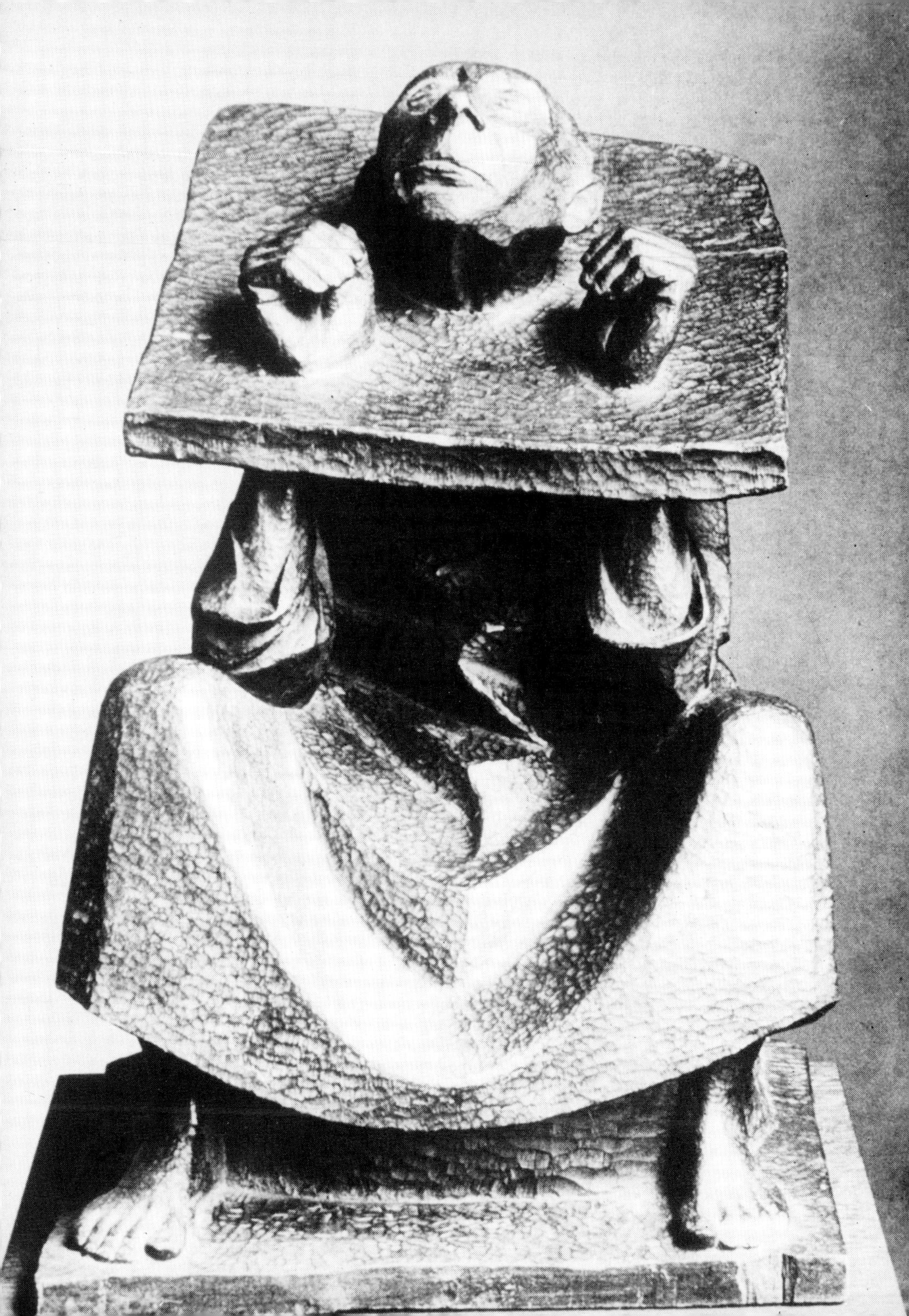

I am like a man in love who longs to
adore his creator; my sense of sight
and touch, my whole capacity to feel
reaches out in adoration and gratitude;
so I direct this gratitude towards
the creation in which as in a
sacrament I am given a visible
manifestation.

One must not try to puzzle it out;
one must just believe and in doing
so one gets free from oneself ...
Consciousness is let go. I am like
a horse without a halter on the
pastures of infinity.

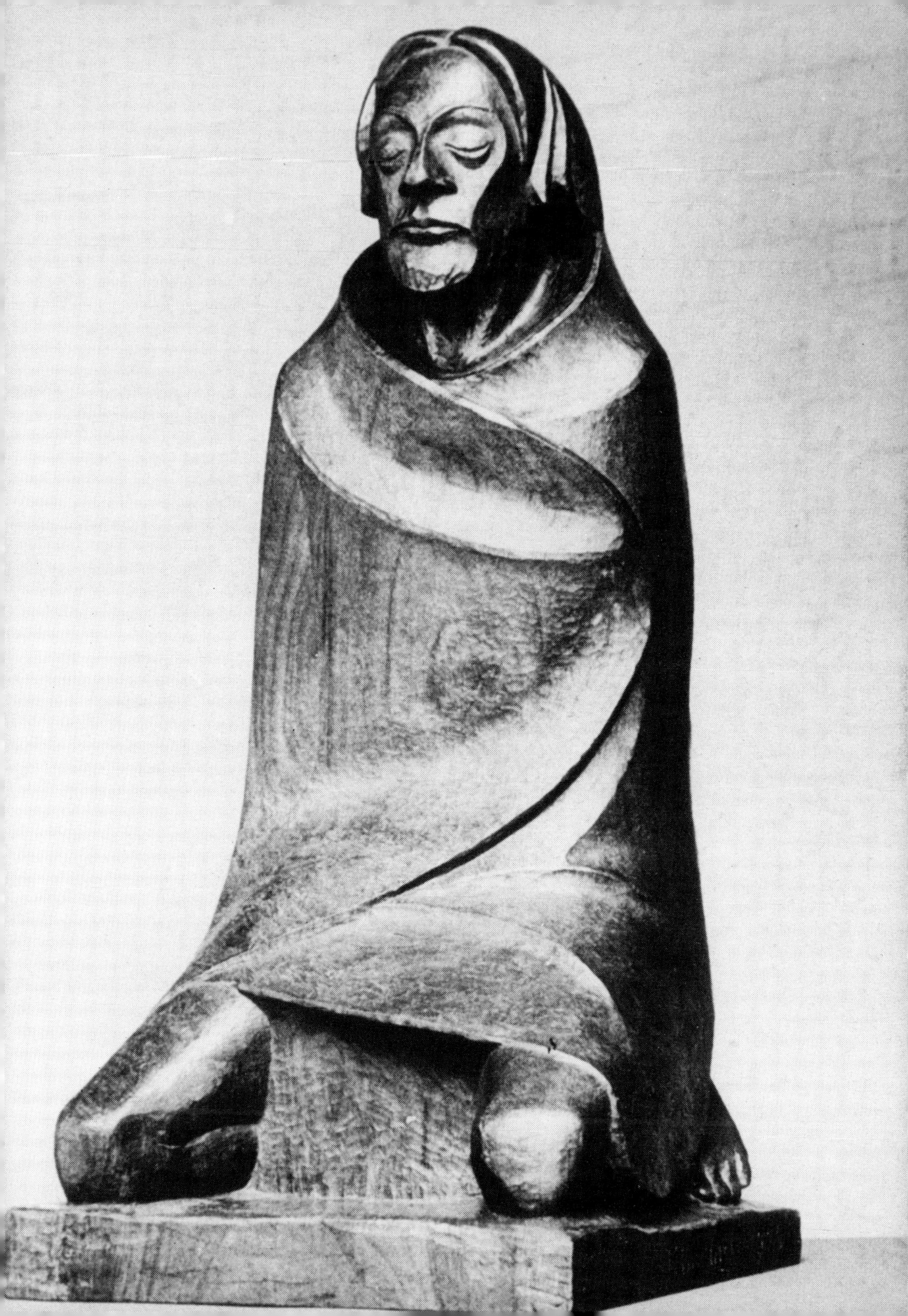

Creation has no end. Ultimately the
creator and the creature are one ...
This force in us is the force of God,
in everything — all our labours, our
longings, our struggles, our hopes,
our achievements, our joys and our
angers ... Art and music sometimes
give us a glimpse of undiscovered worlds.

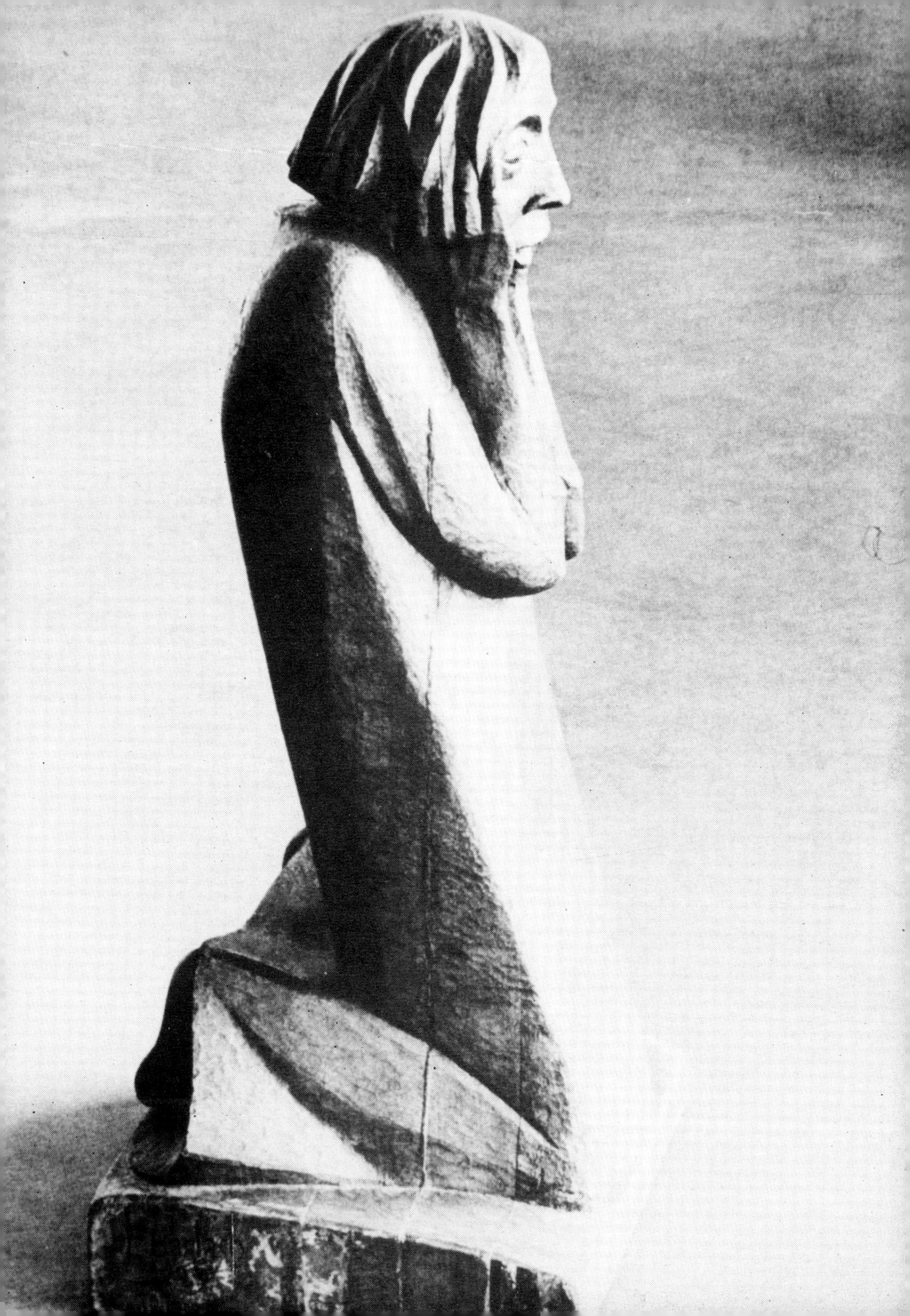

In that he is driven totally to live out
his humanity, to suffer it through, and
because his sensitivity is sharpened to
suffer it all the more deeply, to live it
more seriously, more profoundly because
of that sharpening — that is what makes
a man an artist.

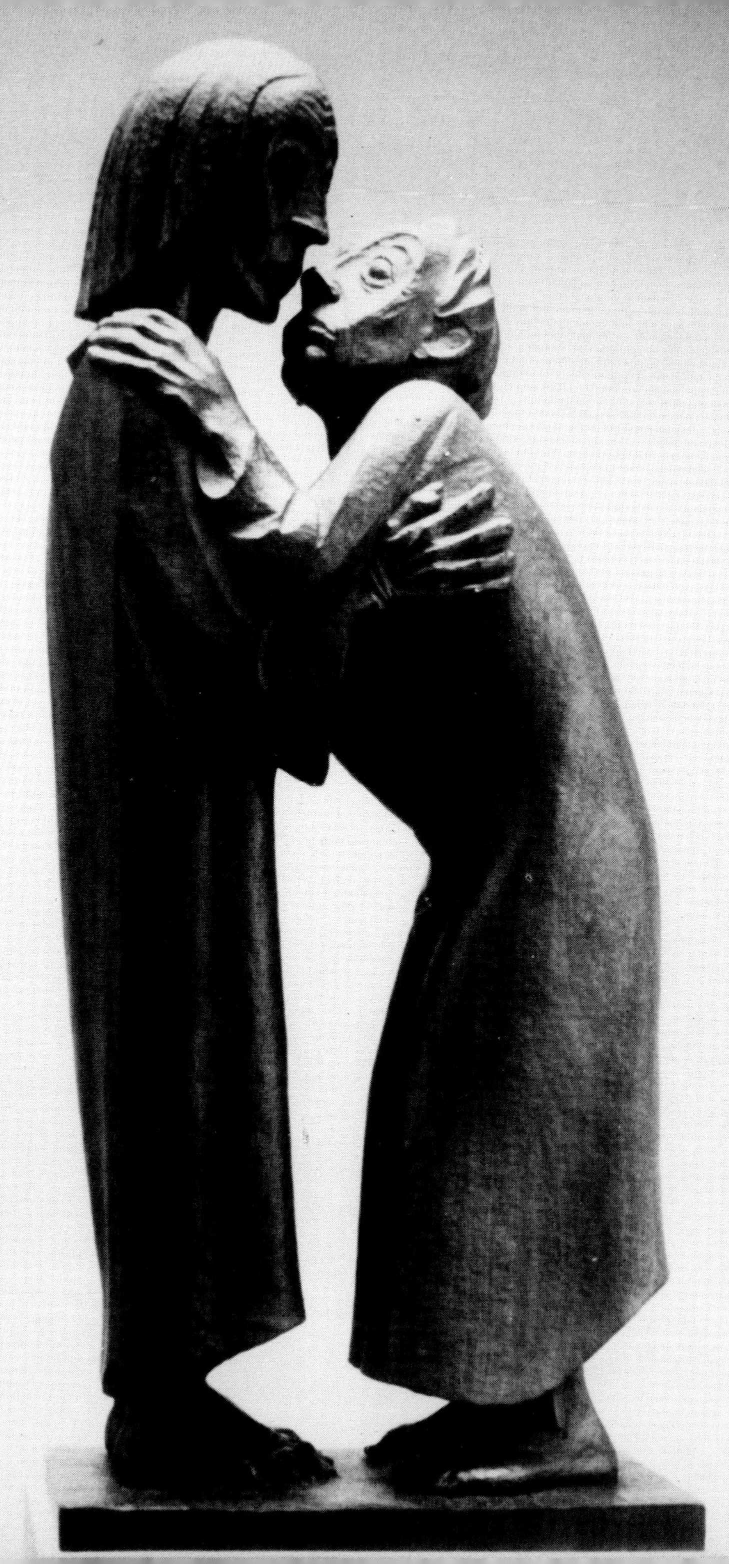

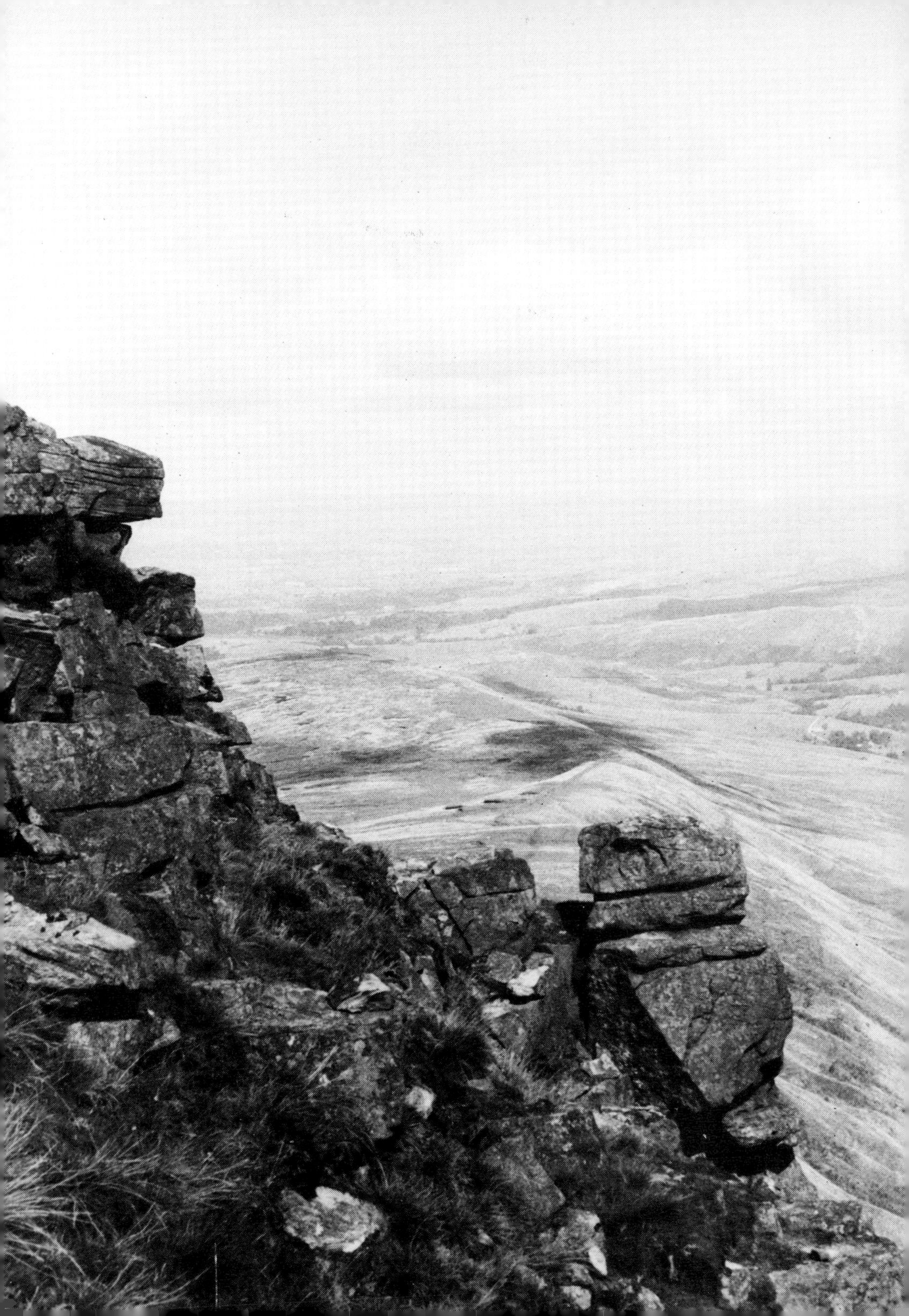

BARBARA HEPWORTH

I think the very nature of art
is affirmative, and in being so
it reflects the laws and the
evolution of the universe.

Rock and metal: these are the basic stuff of which the earth is built. What do we do with them?

The exploration of the world's resources for our own purposes is something that to-day we take for granted. We have lost the habit of looking at things for their own natural qualities. To enable us to see the world as a gift, to be accepted with gratitude and used with reverence, we need the artist.

Barbara Hepworth was born and brought up in Yorkshire. "Moving through and over the West Riding landscape with my father in his car, the hills were sculptures; the roads defined the form. Above all there was the sensation of moving physically over the contours of fullnesses and concavities, through hollows and over peaks — feeling, touching, seeing through mind and hand and eye."

Long ago the Christian Church took some of the basic elements of our day-to-day life — water, bread, wine — to symbolize certain spiritual realities. Art is not meant to be a substitute for the sacraments, but perhaps a sculptor who uses in her work the common materials of the everyday world — stone, metal, glass — and explores their possibilities can help us to have through them a new sense of the transcendent. We may even begin to find these simple forms expressing for us deep levels of experience that we find difficult to put into words.

Born in Wakefield in 1903, Barbara Hepworth went on to study at Leeds College of Art, where Henry Moore was a fellow-student. Later after travelling in Italy — "Florence, Siena, Lucca, Arezzo, basking in the new bright light" — she settled in London with her husband Ben Nicholson and a group of fellow artists which at one time included Naum Gabo. From there she moved to St. Ives in Cornwall, where she died in 1975.

Cornwall with its long curves of moorland, its standing stones and caves coiled into cliffs, provided new imagery; so did the rhythms of the sea, the spirals in shells, the pattern and structure of crystals. Forms and relationships, spaces between forms, the space inside caves, holes and hollows in rocks became very important. For her they were "a piercing of the superficial surfaces of material existence." It is as though we are invited to climb into these sculptures and explore them, and so to look out with fresh vision on earth and the mystery and meaning within it.

In these new experiences of the world around her she found inspiration for work which may have little to do with traditional religious symbolism but often expresses, in her own words, "a rhythm of form which has its roots in earth but reaches outwards towards the unknown experiences of the future."

The idea — the imaginative concept —
actually *is* the giving of life and vitality to material.

Vitality is not a physical, organic attribute of sculpture:
it is a spiritual inner life.

Power is not man power or physical capacity:
it is an inner force and energy.

Vision is not sight:
it is the perception of the mind.

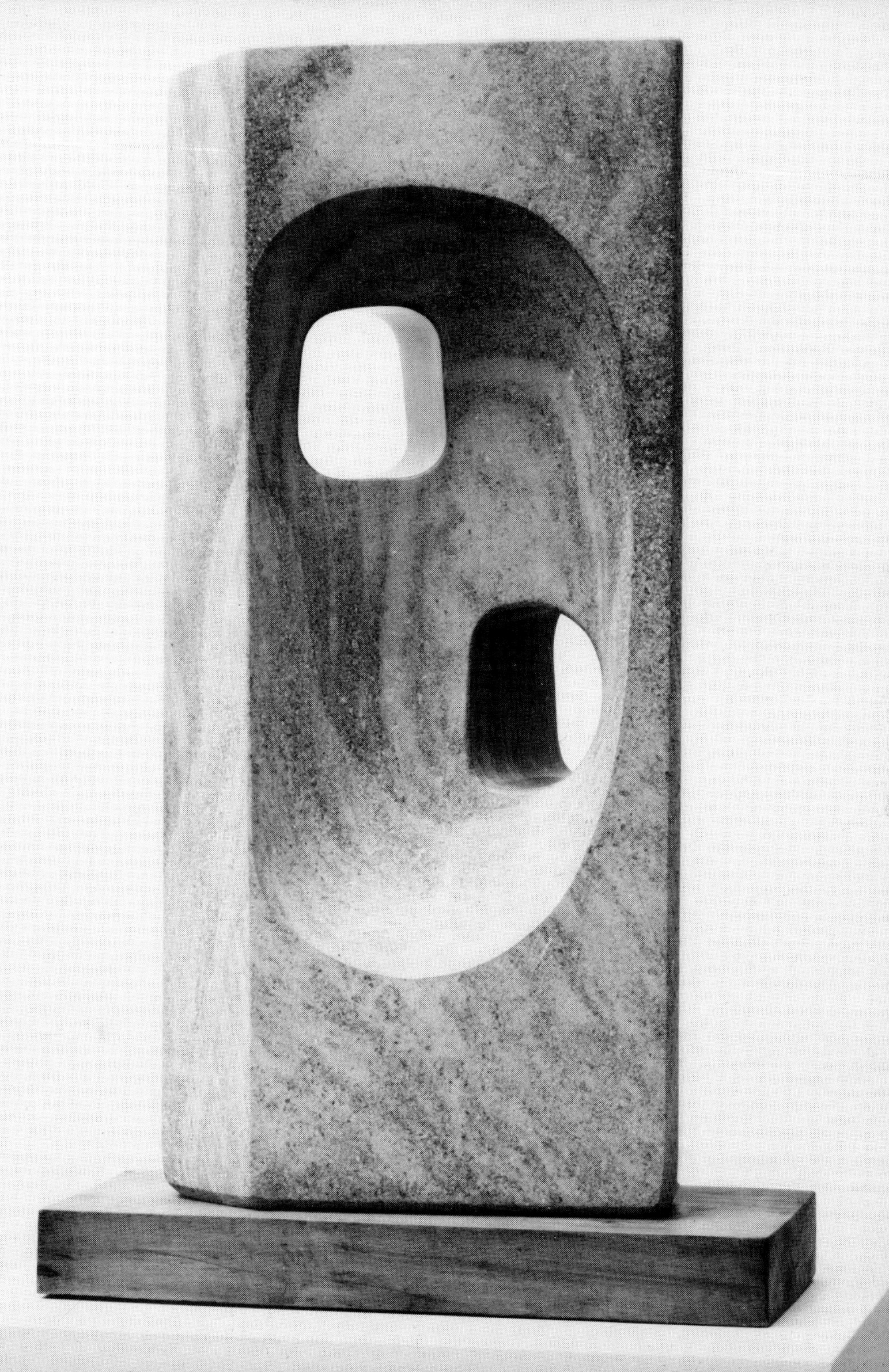

There is an inside and an outside to
every form. When they are in special
accord, as for instance a nut in its
shell, a child in the womb, or in the
structure of shells or crystals, or
when one senses the architecture of
bones in the human figure, then I am
most drawn to the effect of light.
Every shadow cast by the sun from an
ever-varying angle reveals the harmony
of the inside and outside.

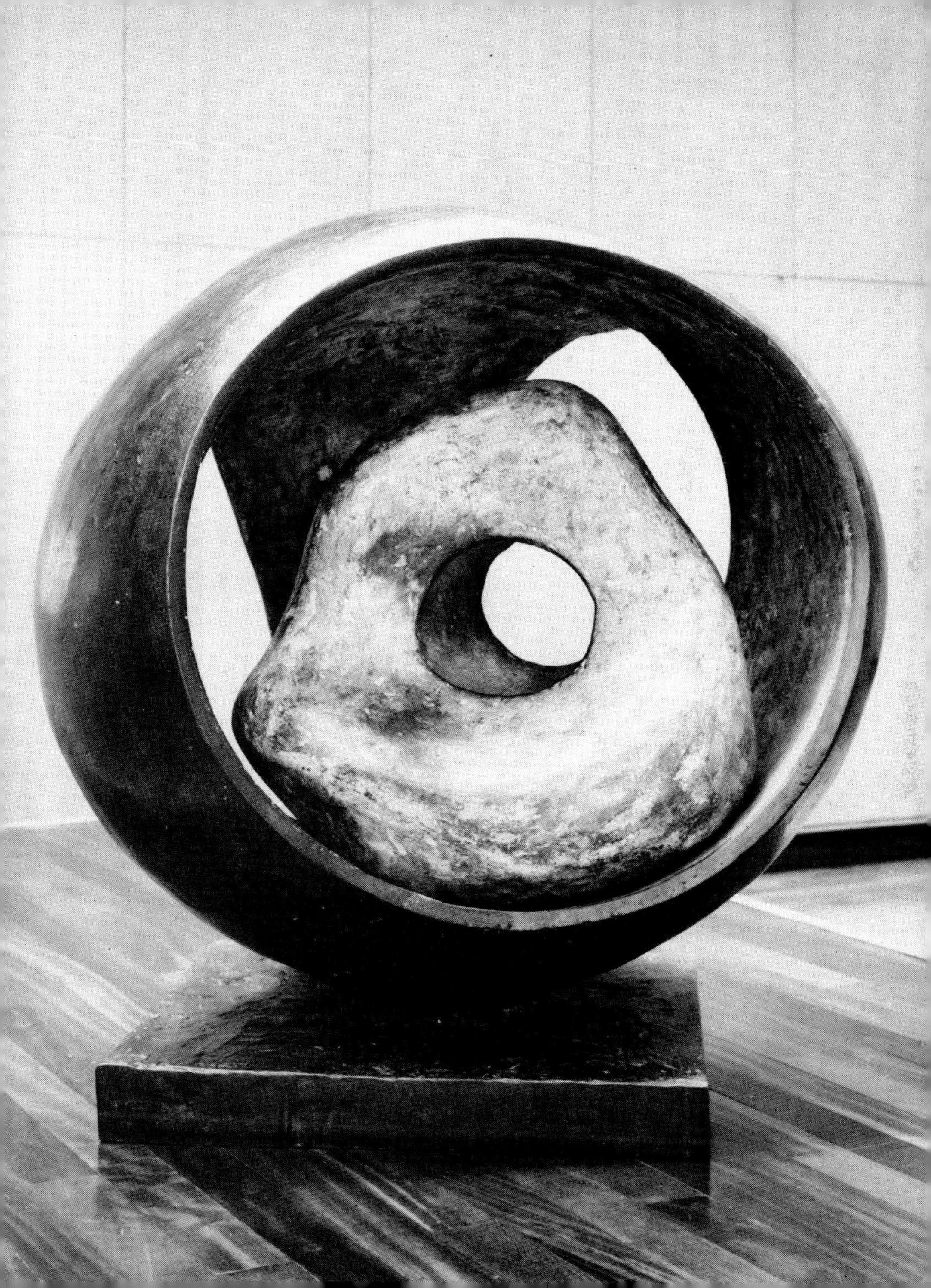

Working in the abstract way seems to
release one's personality and sharpen the
perceptions.

The components fall into place and one is
no longer aware of the detail except as
the necessary significance of wholeness
and unity.

The thought underlying this form is, for
me, the delicate balance the spirit of
man maintains between his knowledge
and the laws of the universe.

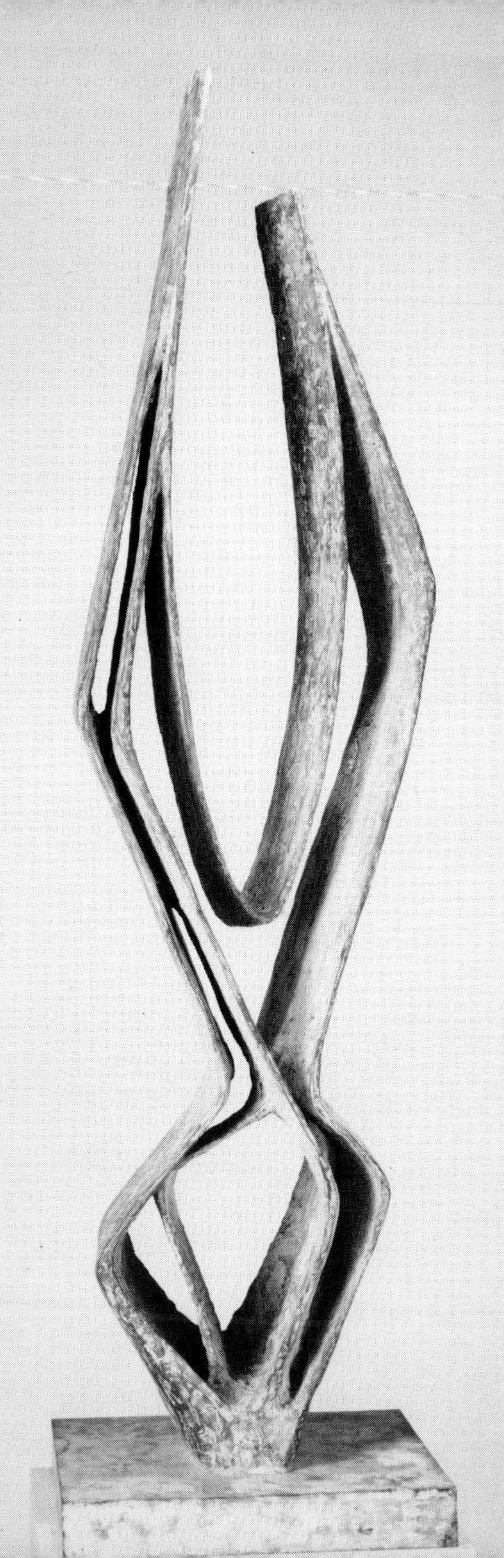

The artist rebels against the world as he
finds it because his sensibility reveals to
him a world that could be possible.

It is the discernment of the reality of
life, a piercing of the superficial
surfaces of material existence, that gives
a work of art its own life and purpose
and significant power.

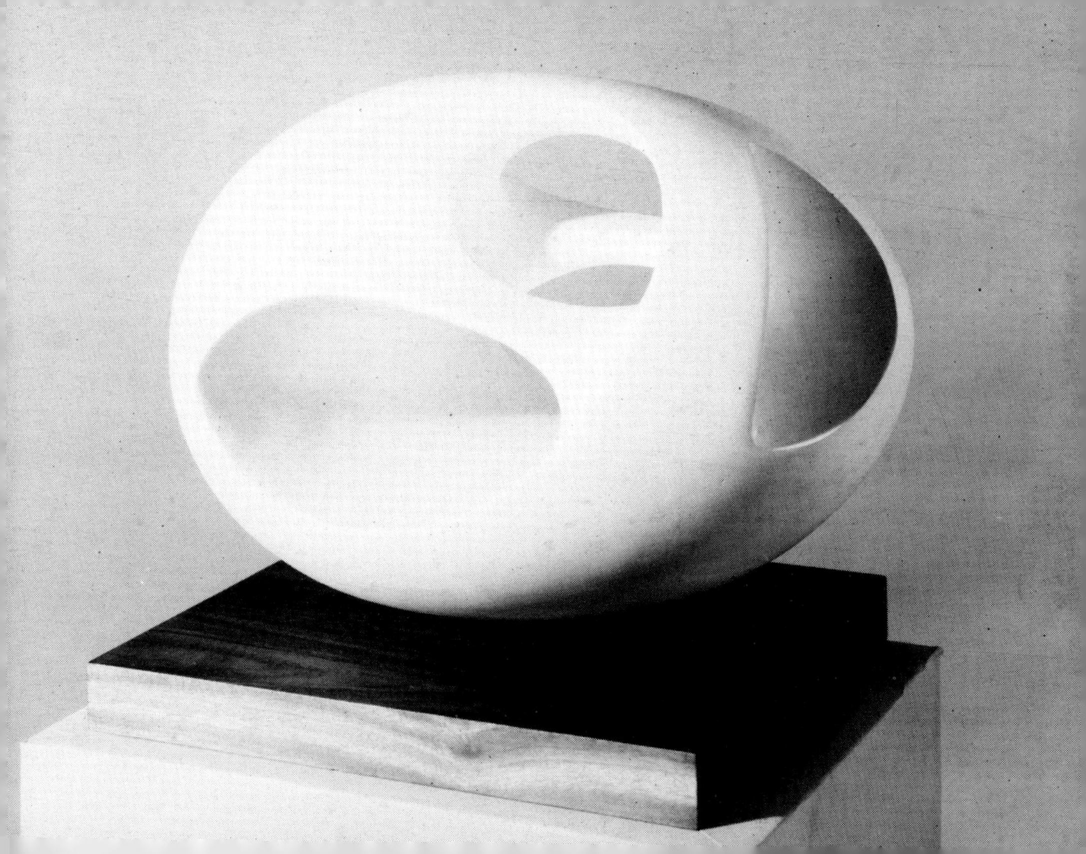

The artist works because he must! But he
learns by the disciplines of his imagination.

Through moments of ecstasy or great despair,
when all thoughts of self are lost, a work
seems to evolve which has not only the vivid
uniqueness of a new creation, but also the
seeming effortlessness and unalterable
simplicity of a true idea relating to the
universe.

In our present time, so governed by fear of
destruction, the artist senses more and more
the energies and impulses which give life and
are the affirmation of life.

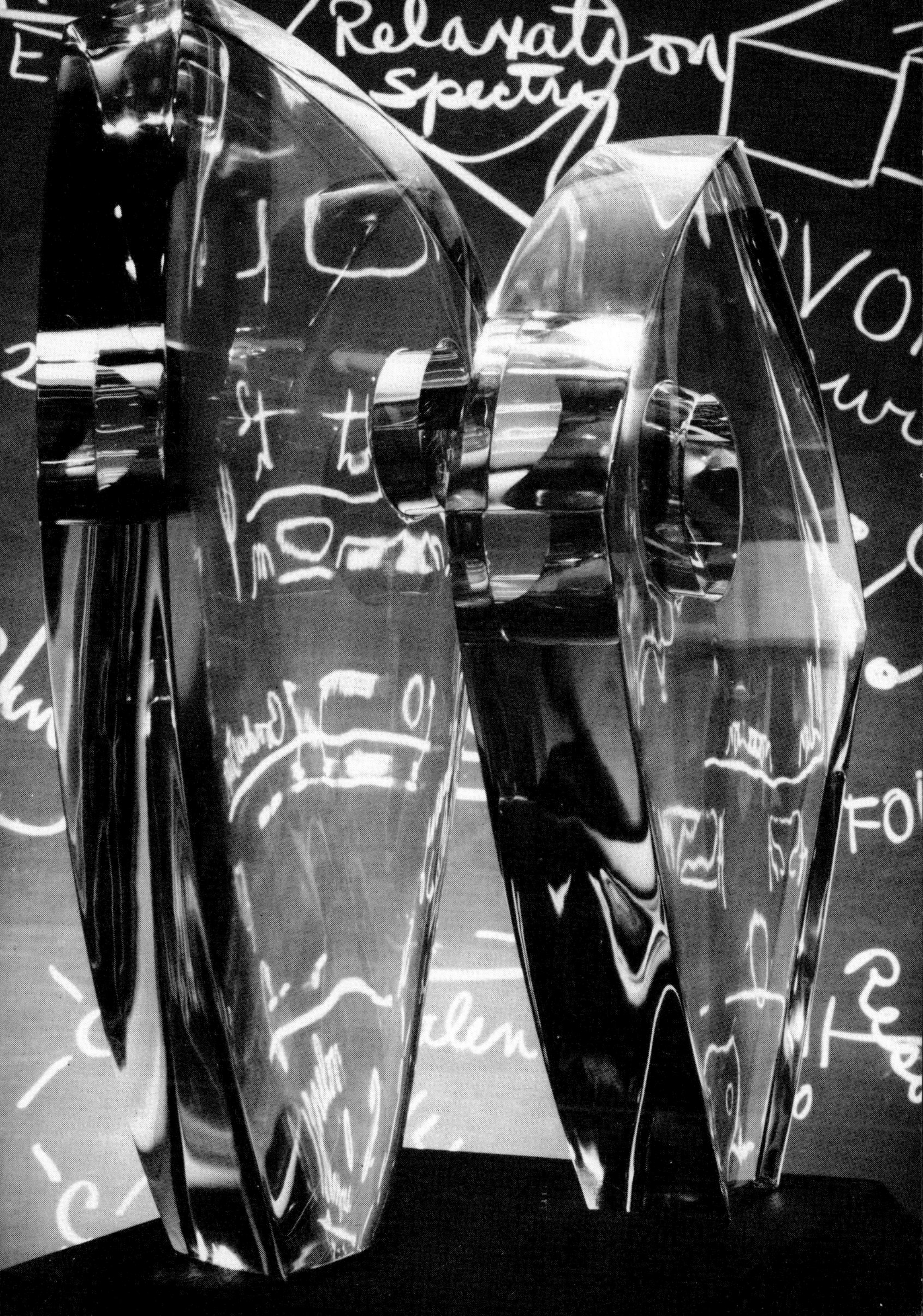

Relaxation
Spectra

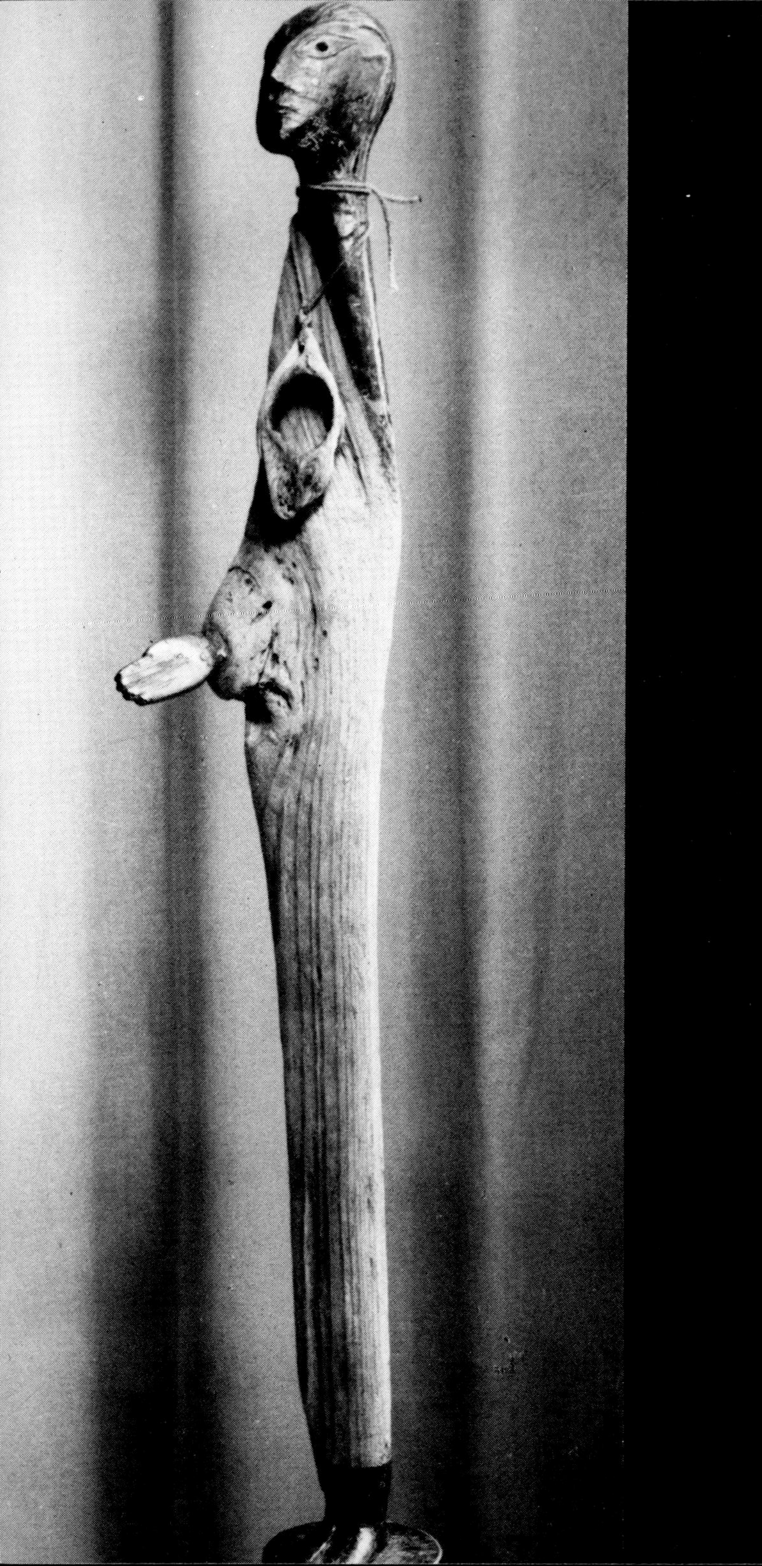

PETER EUGENE BALL

Whether we be young or old,
Our destiny, our being's heart and home,
Is with infinitude, and only there;
With hope it is, hope that can never die,
Effort, and expectation, and desire,
And something evermore about to be.

"I think art has a purely spiritual significance", Peter Ball says. "I don't use that word in any religious way. I just use it of a kind of experience that's on a different plane from ordinary experience. Yet it can reflect ordinary experience too — as religion does. In fact the more you think about it, the more similar they are, art and religion I mean."

To suggest this experience that is on a different plane from the ordinary, Peter Ball uses the most ordinary material. Not ordinary, though, for the sculptor. Much of it in fact has already been put to use for some other purpose. All the work illustrated here, for example, makes some use of driftwood — scraps of timber picked up on the sea shore. From these the perpetual movement of wave and tide has worn away all the softer parts, smoothing off the rough edges and leaving only the bare bones of the tree, the hard grain, the indestructible core. Going into the sea was for this wood a kind of death; finding a new life as a work of art has been a kind of resurrection.

Peter Ball was born in 1943, and worked for a time in the car industry in the Midlands before becoming a full-time sculptor in 1971. His skill in metal-work is combined with a profound respect for the materials he uses. "The sculptor must be honest to the stone, the wood, or whatever it is. These pieces of driftwood, they're still driftwood; yet they also represent something else. The important thing is not to destroy that original nature, as driftwood."

These figures do not belong to any particular time or place. Sometimes they come out of the Christian tradition; more often they are neither ancient nor modern, timeless representatives of the human race as it always has been, always will be: universal types of humanity.

And God? "There's no mystery left these days", says Peter Ball. "How can there be a God any more? People have just intellectualized Him out of existence."

So what can the artist do? What we see in these sculptures is a stripping away of all the superficial detail by which we form our first judgements of people — indications of social status, education, income, intellectual achievement, even religion — till nothing is left but the bare human soul, in all its dignity and misery, undefeated, questioning, searching. They may remind us that when all that seems to make life worth living is taken from us, life itself may be not poorer but richer for the loss.

"The deepest truth I have discovered is that if one accepts the loss, if one gives up clinging to what is irretrievably gone, then the nothing which is left is not barren but enormously fruitful. Everything that one has lost comes flooding back again out of the darkness, and one's relation to it is new — free and unclinging. But the richness of the nothing contains far more, it is the all-possible, it is the spring of freedom. In that sense the faith of loss is closer to joy than to despair."

They're very quiet, these
figures, aren't they? They
don't shout at you. It's as
though they were mutes. This
silence, I think it's something
very important, more important
than any statement. They may
not speak, but you're aware of
something coming from them all
the time. Jesus was like that,
presumably. Without his even
speaking there was that presence.
People were awed by it.

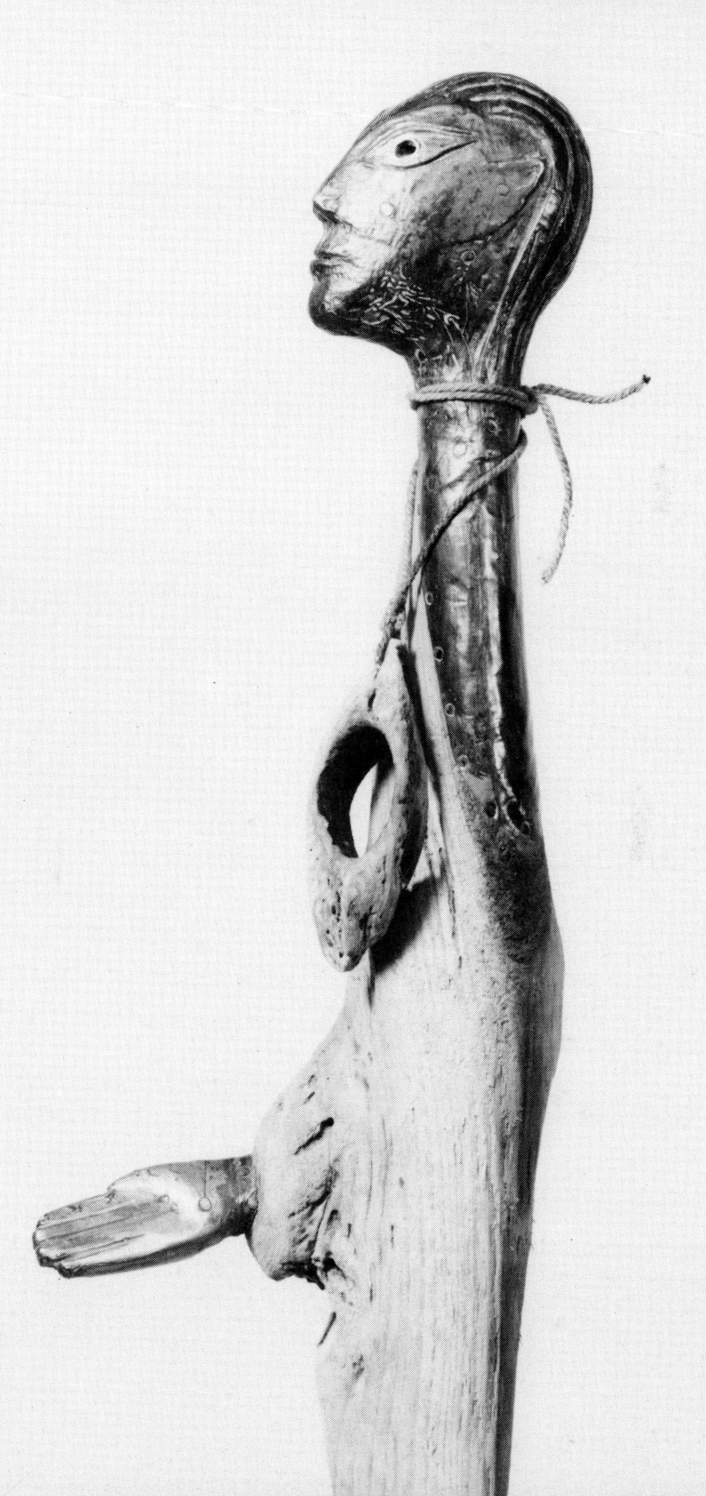

Man hath still either toys or care,
He hath no root, nor to one place is tied,
But ever restless and irregular
    About this earth doth run and ride;
He knows he hath a home but scarce knows where,
        He says it so far
That he hath quite forgot how to go there.

He knocks at all doors, strays and roams,
Nay, hath not so much wit as some stones have
Which in the darkest nights point to their homes,
    By some hid sense their Maker gave;
Man is the shuttle, to whose winding quest
        And passage through these looms
God ordered motion, but ordained no rest.

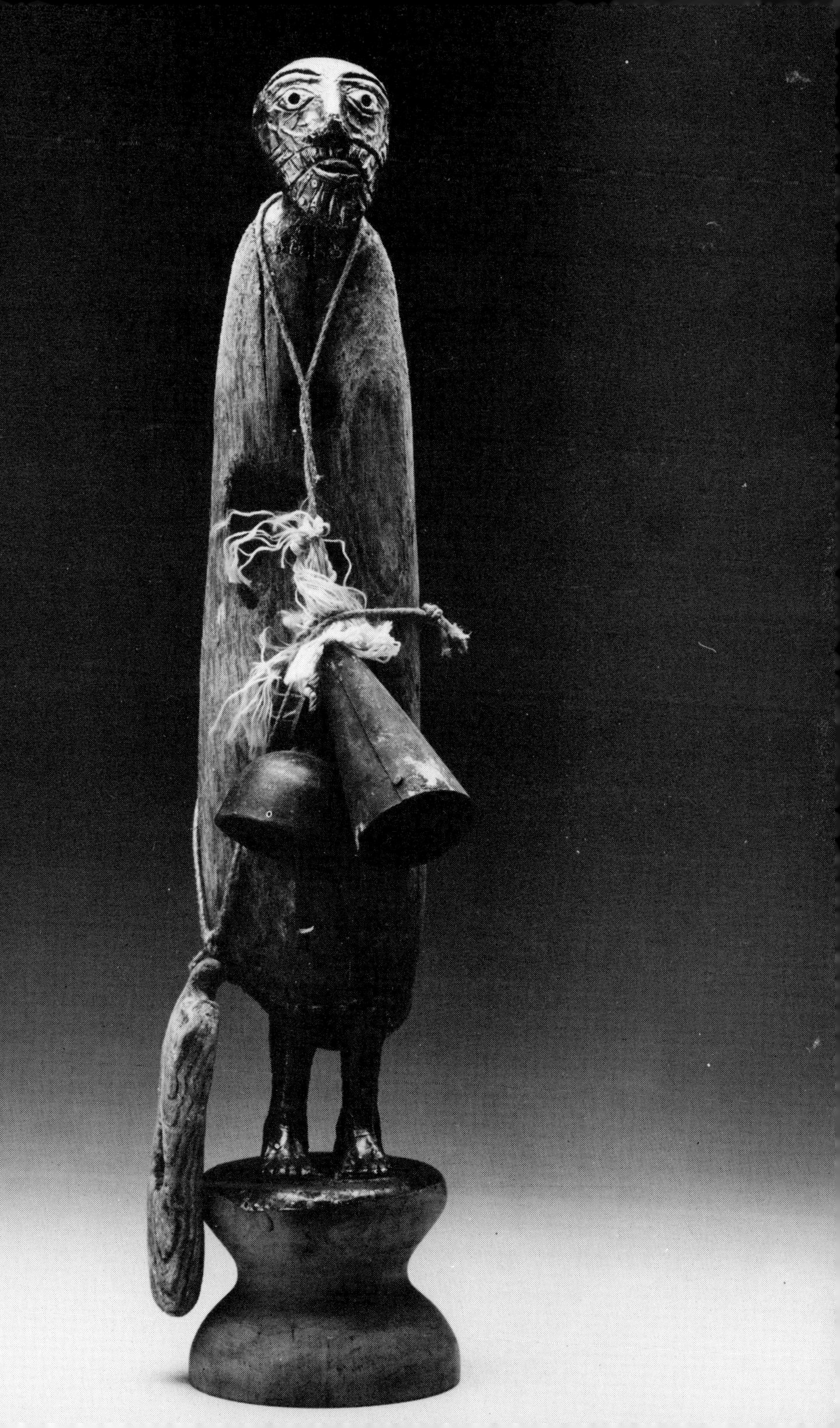

Each of these pieces of driftwood has
been through so many lives, first as a
tree, then as part of a ship or whatever — and now it has a new kind of
life, as a work of art. It is a
fascinating thing that a piece of wood
designed with one function in mind
should end up serving a quite different
function — a spiritual one. This is a
function absolutely essential in any
society. It may be dead, this piece of
wood I mean, but what's left of it has a
new kind of life of its own: there's a
sort of timelessness about it.

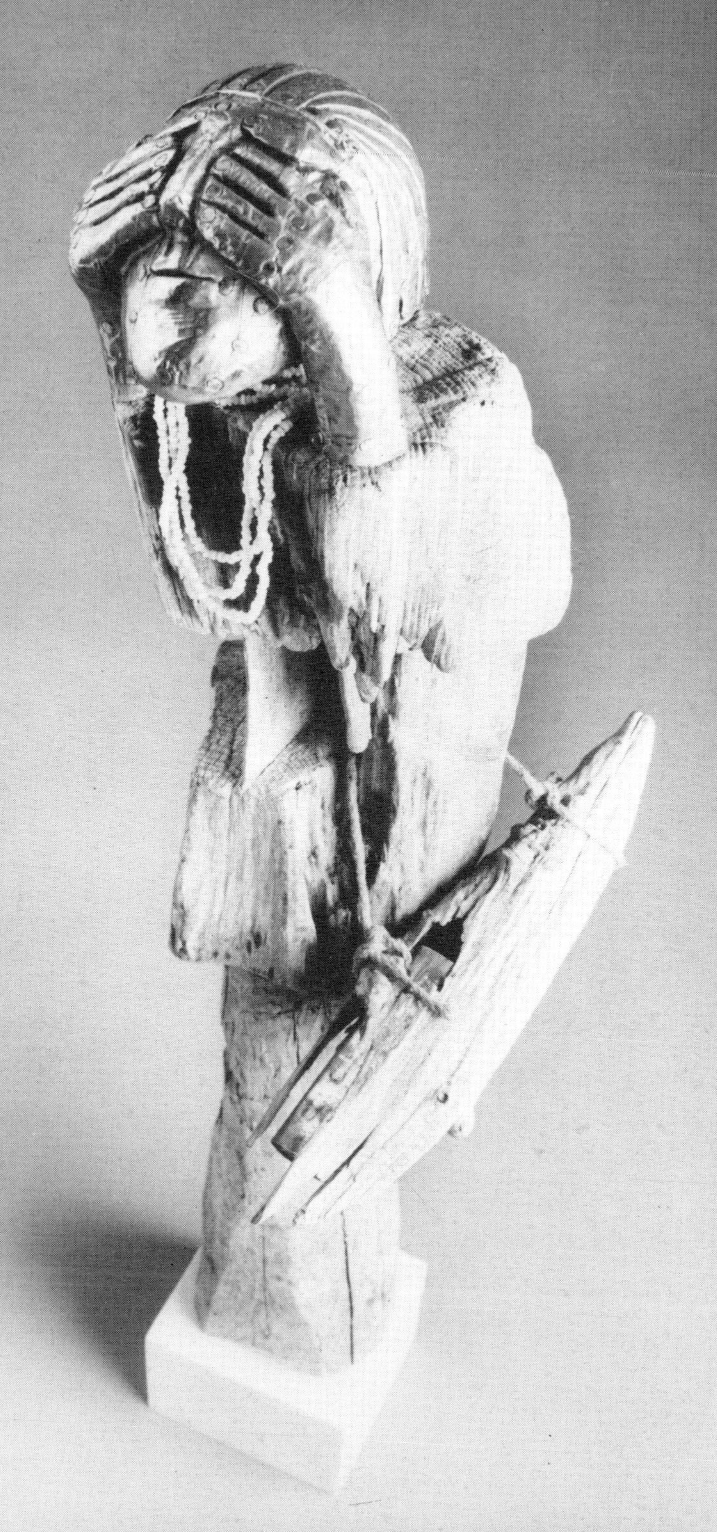

I've always been interested
in a Christ that's compassionate yet aloof; not quite
involved with humanity yet
representing them. To me
this is not an agonized Christ
but very calm; compassionate
but resigned.

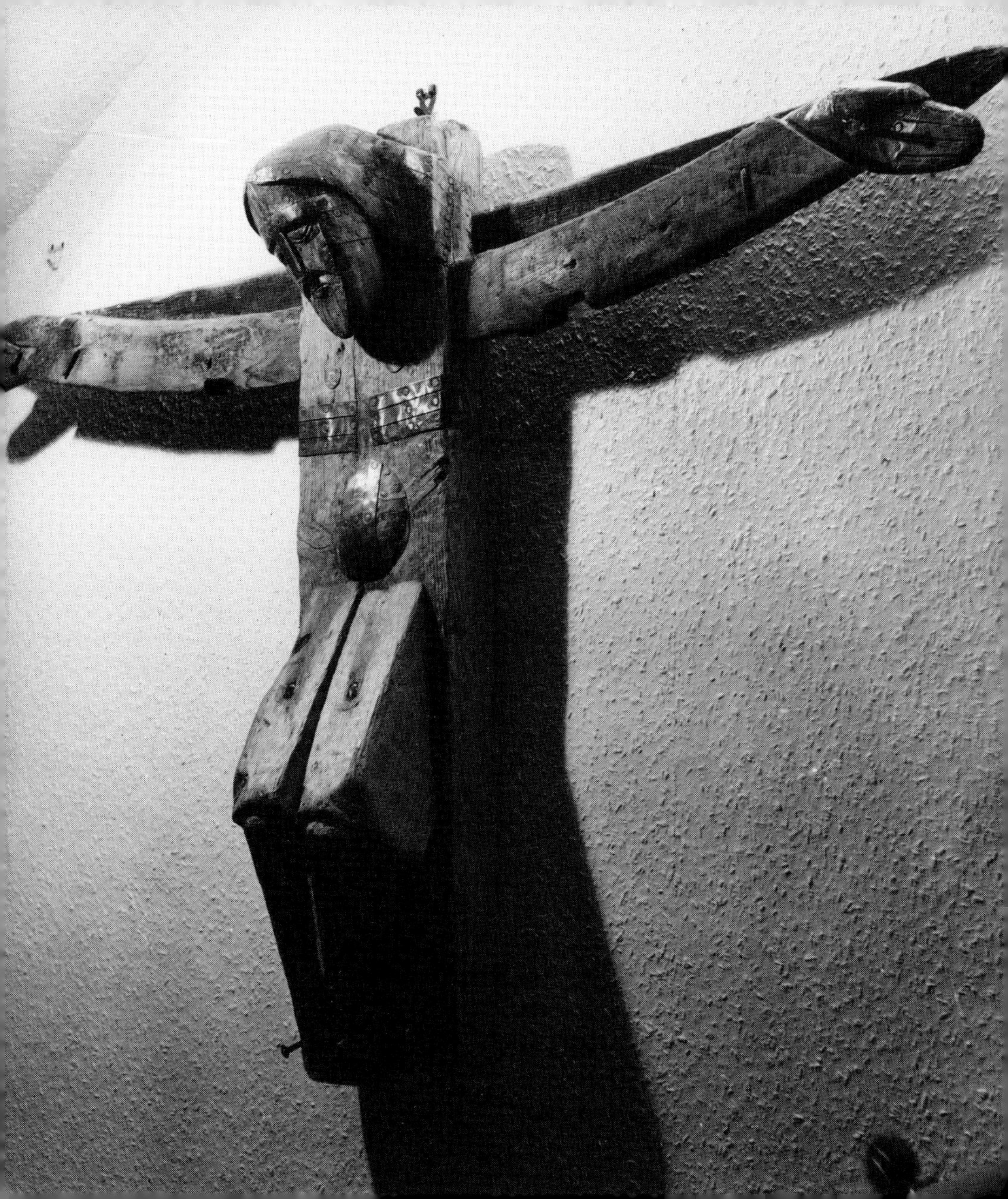

This detachment, it's a way of coping;
recognizing human pain and suffering
but not being destroyed by it. After
all, you can't offer anybody anything
if you're destroyed by what you see,
can you? There's lots of suffering
in the world, there are lots of poor
people, there are millions of people
starving all over the world. Yet
before you can come to terms with
all this, you have to be aloof,
detached from it. Then perhaps you
may be able to give something back.

There's something of this in the
Christ there. In a way he's saying,
"I'm finished with you"; and yet
he's also saying, "I'm giving you
hope, this hasn't destroyed me."
That's what it's about.

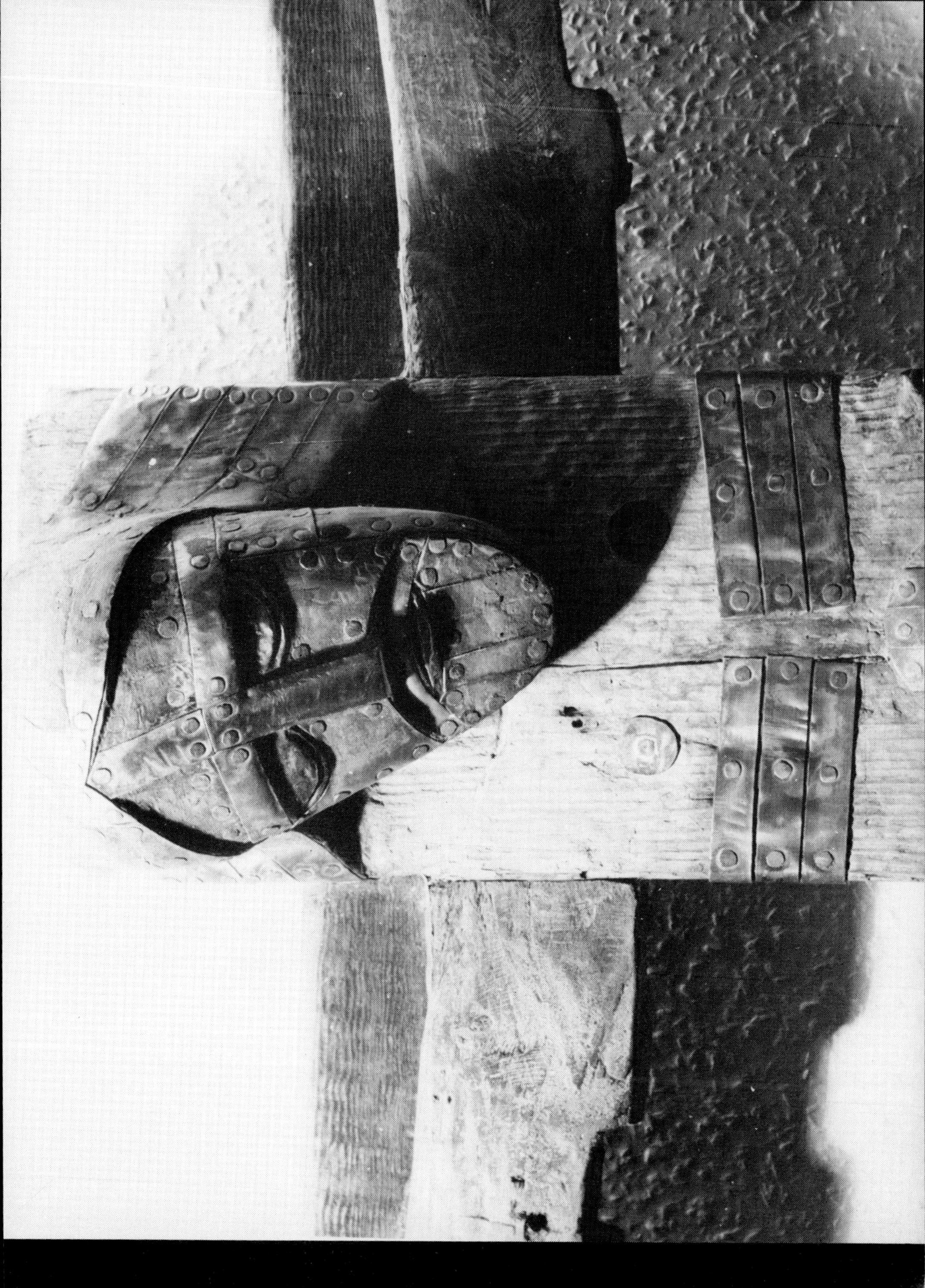

Notes on the Text

p. 7:   *Art is an attempt* ... Simone Weil, *Forms of the Implicit Love of God,* in *Waiting on God,* trans. Emma Craufurd (Collins, Fontana Books, London, 1959), p. 123.

p. 8:   *We shall never have to undertake* ... Naum Gabo, *The Constructive Idea in Art,* in *Circle,* ed. Martin, Nicholson & Gabo (Faber, London, 1937). p. 9.

p. 9:   *Across the ashes and cindered homes* ... Naum Gabo, *The Realistic Manifesto,* 1920, in Stephen Bann (ed.) *The Tradition of Constructivism* (Thames & Hudson, London, 1974), pp. 5ff.
A world at war, it seems to me ... Naum Gabo, Letter to Herbert Read, 1942, published in *Horizon* (London), Vol.X, No. 53, July 1944.

pp. 10, 12, 14, 16, 18:
Naum Gabo, Letter to Herbert Read.

p. 21:   *I can trust my senses* ... Ernst Barlach, Letter to Fraulein N.N., 23 Sept. 1915.

p. 22:   *My mother tongue* ... Ernst Barlach, Letter of 1911, in C.D. Carls, *Ernst Barlach* (Pall Mall Press, London, 1969) p. 9.
I can bid goodbye to everything ... Ernst Barlach, op.cit., p. 41.
I have for a long time now ... Ernst Barlach, Letter to Wolf-Dieter Zimmerman, 12 Feb. 1935.

p. 24:   *Joy as content, purpose, meaning* ... Ernst Barlach, commenting on his nine woodcuts of 1927 on Schiller's *Ode to Joy,* in op.cit., p. 147.

p. 26;   From the records of the Religious Experience Research Unit: a man is describing an experience that happened to him at the age of 20. See Edward Robinson, *Living the Questions* (Studies in Religious Experience, Manchester College, Oxford, 1979), pp. 121ff.

p. 28:   *I am like a man in love* ... Ernst Barlach, Letter to Fraulein N.N., 23 Sept. 1915.

p. 30:   *Creation has no end* ... Ernst Barlach, Letter to Karl Barlach, 17 Aug. 1931.

p. 32:   *In that he is driven totally* ... Ernst Barlach, Letter to Wolf-Dieter Zimmermann, 12 Feb. 1935.

p. 35:   *I think the very nature of art* ... Barbara Hepworth, *A Pictorial Autobiography* (Moonraker Press, Bradford-on-Avon, 1970), p. 24.

p. 36:   *Moving through and over the West Riding* ... Barbara Hepworth, *A Pictorial Autobiography,* p. 9.

p. 38:   *The idea — the imaginative concept* ... Barbara Hepworth, *Sculpture,* in *Circle,* ed. Martin, Nicholson & Gabo (Faber, London, 1937), p. 113.

p. 40:   *There is an inside and an outside* ... Barbara Hepworth, *A Pictorial Autobiography,* p. 27.

p. 42:   *Working in the abstract way* ... Barbara Hepworth, *A Pictorial Autobiography,* p. 93.

p. 44:   *The artist rebels against the world* ... Barbara Hepworth, in *Circle,* p. 116.

p. 46:   *The artist works because he must* ... Barbara Hepworth, *A Pictorial Autobiography,* p. 24.

p. 49:   *Whether we be young or old* ... Wordsworth, *The Prelude,* Book 6, 603.

pp. 50, 52, 56, 58, 60:
All the quotations on these pages are taken from a recorded and unpublished conversation between Peter Eugene Ball and Edward Robinson of April 1980.

p. 51:   *The deepest truth I have discovered* ... Robert Bellah, *Beyond Belief* (Harper & Row, New York, 1970), pp. xxf.

p. 54:   Henry Vaughan, *Man.*